A Pair of Glasses
And their
Brown Trouser
Moments

David Glass

DAVID GLASS

ISBN-13: 978-1539614333

ISBN-10: 1539614336

DEDICATION

I feel there are so many people I have met in my life that have in some way helped with this book. That said I do not want to fill a book up with just names, and if I missed anyone I am truly sorry.

To My Soul Mate Elizabeth Ann

CONTENTS

ACKNOWLEDGMENTS

So many to thank for their help, I guess a big thank you to all those that have joined my Facebook page Brown Trouser Moment Camping with Nan.

A big thank you to Carol Dent, who has helped me run this page, next Julie Game, because without you this would never have become a book.

On a personal level I would like to thank my stomach for hating me so much - without it this would only be half the tale it is.

And lastly to my long suffering northern ice queen and soul mate Elizabeth.

MEET NAN OUR ELDERLY CAMPERVAN

A few months ago, I was driving home from work and saw a camper for sale, I pulled over and went for a nosey. It turned out to be a 1982 Bedford CF called Nan. I loved her lines and what the owners had done to the inside was amazing, anyway after a few months of the owners being messed around by time wasters Nan finally end up ours. I took her home and spent the next few weeks sorting a few things out (timing, table, adjusting the bed lay out and buying camping stuff). The day neared when we would get to use her!!!! The night before we opened a road atlas and the wife pointed with her claw (I meant nail) to Wales...then to Bala...we searched t'internet, found a site and booked a night as a test run.

The next day fully loaded I started her up, now she's old and her ignition barrel was broken in the past so to start her you have to press and click several different switches to get her going (just like a really women I hear you say....) to me it felt like I was starting a Spitfire and I shot off the drive shouting like Mel Gibson in Braveheart, only with better hair and makeup "FREEDOM!!!"

As we made our way to the motorway we soon discovered she had what I can only describe as teenager brakes you know the ones...no matter how much you shout, scream or push, you only get a sigh and little to no effort to the task set them. With a bum like a rabbits nose we continued on to the motorway, where to our shock Nan started to flirt with any truck or van passing us by swaying her back end about (how embarrassing!).

As we left the main roads to deepest darkest Wales we soon discovered Nan didn't like corners and we often found ourselves on the wrong side of the road, much to the horror of other oncoming motor homers (I am so sorry if any were you but we did wave!!!) up the hills she needed a Stannah stair lift. We also discovered that unlike my Nan who only sipped the sherry this Nan drank like a condemned man at a free bar. Our satnav (we now call Garmin Death wish 2000) took us down roads that got thinner, trees got lower until the path left was only suitable for a stunt mountain goat (with a death wish!!).

After three hours of brown trouser moments we arrived at our site to be met by a person I am sure was Wales' lemon sucking champion 1969. We paid our fee and moved to our pitch right on the side of the lake no less. We pulled up and unpacked...oh how my wife howled at me fighting the hook up cable. As my wife put the kettle on and let the dogs out (on the lead before you all start) the rain started and didn't stop till we got home, it was awesome!!! Our Nan might be old but she gives us such great times, memories and smiles...well that was my 1st outing how bad was yours?

SPIDERNAN

Here is a vision for you...imagine a fifteen stone bloke hunched over his ample driver belly, his face screwed up in concentration (my wife likens it to a Buddha with constipation), tongue stuck out to the left, slowly typing out these tales of woe. The sound effects if you need these to add to your mental image are of loud straining grunts, tuts and growls along with a healthy amount of swearing, as his ideas flow faster than his solitary finger can punch them into his computer.

This chapter is about the days leading up to Bala. It is a long one, my tendency is to ramble...you will get used to this. Having just purchased Nan and brought her home, over the next few days we set about making her better suited to the needs of only two people and two dogs.

Removing the van seats fitted to carry more people by the previous owners, just in case our daughter has any mad ideas about joining us.

That week I worked in the day and mostly, just sat in Nan of an evening getting to know her, a little overawed that she had become mine, and toying with the fact that Nan came with a four seater table. You know the unstable ones with straight bits of metal sticking out dangerously at right angles, the wobbly ones that rock and roll, making eating on them an art form because your food slides back and forth as you attempt to eat it, the ones no-one puts their drink on without expecting to wear it?

3

Having set it up to see how it all looked, it seemed every time I wanted to get up, me being the size I am ended up doing an impression of that 70's disco hit by the Bee Gees. You know the one 'Ha Ha Ha Ha stayin' alive, stayin' alive'. In my mind's eye I would like to think I looked like John Travolta but that is too far a stretch even for my imagination...with the added hazard of Gorgeous George under the table trying to trip me up for his own muttley entertainment. There was no way I was going to chance it, it was no good it had to go.

When I finished work on the Friday I was dragged into the office and informed that my thirteen week trial period had ended, they had been so impressed they wanted to take me on...great!!! Things were really going my way. But No!! (Fate being the fickle lady she is, played her hand). As the transport manager told me of my new hourly wage, I started laughing, tears rolling down my face, I pointed at him and sticking my thumb up trying to say... you told a funny....go you.... trying to get my breath back I leaned back so far on the chair, it toppled over and for five minutes I could not get back up again for laughing at the insulting sum (5k less a year). How was I to know he was being serious? Needless to say I was politely asked to leave and told never to comeback.

One memory that has just sprung to mind from when I worked for this company (and while it does not have anything to do with campervans - I still feel it is in some way relevant as all campervans have to be driven and there is a good chance that you will meet one of these characters on your travels). It was a particular drop, that I hated doing the most, on an industrial estate situated on the outskirts of Desborough Northamptonshire. It wasn't the customer or the large amounts they ordered I disliked, but rather the tightness of the road I had to use getting in and out. You know the type of street with cars abandoned on either side, the road that only a bicycle can get down never mind a 7.5 ton truck? I am sure you have probably already found yourselves on similar ones.

On this particular day I was threading my lorry through, and cars coming the opposite way were graciously giving way into gaps for me. When out of the blue an arrogant, inconsiderate school-run-mum driver with a face that would scare statues into running off, had

4

nothing on her mind but the eager disposal of her child, ignoring the beeping horns, pushed her way down between the waiting cars before coming to a stop practically right against my bumper. She looked up at me with her best... 'it is YOU that is going to move out of MY way' look... Then quickly she moved to the 'Shoo-shoo get out of my way' gesture, when neither of them worked she crossed her arms and set her face with hostile determination. The battle was on.

Now I don't frighten easily out in my native environment, and shackled as I am to a Yorkshire lass, I have long since lost the will to live. So her death stare had no power over me. There was no way this big-ass old truck was moving backwards on this stretch of road anyway so ner! I firmly planted the ball back in her court, as I reached to turn off the ignition, placed my boots on the dash and grabbed my flask. As I sipped my coffee, I fixed her with my best Clint Eastwood steely stare. Like a scene from one of his westerns people started a gathering, mothers grabbed their children behind their skirts, shopkeepers began boarding up... OK OK I'm exaggerating slightly but you are getting the picture no?

After what seemed like an eternity or long enough to finish half a cup of coffee and smoke a cig... the mother from hell, threw up her arms in anguish and crunched her car into reverse. People dived for cover as her Peugeot 308 wheels spun as she shot backwards. Victory was mine... I grinned like a Cheshire cat as I started up my engine and savouring the moment with cheesy grin still in place, I slowly coasted past... Doffing my cap in salute, I drove off into the sun set. Though technically it was sunrise...8:34am to be precise.

Luckily my loyal driving agency came through for me yet again. Monday morning bright and early I was despatched to Ashby-de-la-Zouch I sprang into my wagon and commenced the daily battle with other road users once again. Such is my burden and I face it like the life sentence it is... Finishing early I climbed into my car to race home and as I was coming through Breedon-on-the-Hill, what luck! I spotted a caravan breakers yard! Skidding my car to a halt I jumped out. Hopping and skipping like a child rushing to a candy store, I charged in. Met by a lovely couple, my eyes wide in excitement, I frantically waved my arms about, with spittle flying from my mouth, I described my ideas of what I was wanting to do to my Nan. Clearly uncertain of my intentions towards my aging relative, they stepped back slowly away from the raving loony and gestured over to the row of caravans waiting to be violated mumbling "help yourself".

They stood and watched as what they must have only thought, was the village idiot, run riot round their yard. I soon found the exact thing I was searching for a...double seat that folded into one, unfortunately still attached to its vans floor. Out of nowhere a screwdriver appeared over my shoulder "take it, my wife found you a table to look at too". As I manhandled the seat out of the van and across the yard, his wife lay down the table at my feet with a smile you reserve only for a lunatic. It was perfect. A wall mounted flip-down two person affair. No more looking like I was being electrocuted while trying to get passed the larger table. Whoohoo...I practically drooled as I handed over the money and wedged them into my Micra.

Running in at home I yelled "come and see what I just bought for Nan" before grabbing her keys and fleeing back outside. My wife rolled her eyes and put the kettle on. In a flash I had Nan's backdoor open wide and flinging aside the chair cushions as I lifted the lid on my treasure chest of tools, in eager anticipation....then recoiling in horror as I came-face-to-face with the biggest meanest looking spider I have ever had the displeasure of meeting. Big! Huge!!! I mean it was that huge it was wearing its own Adidas plimsolls and having being disturbed was in the process of pulling on a pair of Lonsdale boxing gloves.

It is here I feel I must add my massive phobia of spiders, yes big brave lorry driving Dave is afraid of teeny-weeny–incy-wincy spiders, even the smallest of money spiders will have me running round in circles meowing like a startled kitten, quite a well-known fact in our street as my screams have brought many a neighbour to my rescue.

Well this thing sent my terror into bowel weakening new heights; I'm talking bottom I'll say no more, I am talking terrapins I'll say no more!!! Snapping turtles!!! Screaming like a little girl I shot into the house. Now my wife can judge the size of a spider by how big the puddle that is developing around my feet, putting the smaller glass away, and squinting at me she selected the largest glass we had and with a sigh marched down the hall and out of the front door.

I promise you on all that is Holy I did try and warn her... but the only noise that I could get out was so high pitched only the dogs understood me and they were cowering in the conservatory. With concern I followed my wife as she stepped up into the backside of Nan, the door slowly swung shut but seconds later my wife flew back out like a human cannon-ball. However in my mind she did look very similar to a witch on a broom. Slamming the door shut and shouting "Oh my God...it is huge Dave." (By the way, I could have thought of a more opportune moment for her to declare this to the whole street - moving swiftly on). All the commotion brought out our neighbour, Glenn an ex-marine of seventy plus years of age. I am completely in awe of this man and have overwhelming admiration for the service he has given our country and the respect he naturally commands. So much so I seem to be unable to communicate with him on an adult level and at best I stammer, stutter and fart my way through any conversations with him like a prat.

With a smirk and a shake of his head he disappeared into the backside of Nan. War cries, crashing, banging, screams of "DIE!!!!" and "COME BACK HERE YOU TWO LEGGED SCOTTISH WUSS!!!" followed by "HA HA IS THAT ALL YA GOT WINCEY!!!" had my wife and I glancing nervously at each other then back to Nan, who was swaying, rocking and looked at one point like she was going to tip over. "Do you think he is OK in there, are you not going in to help?" she asked me "HELL no!" I replied. "I think that bloody spider is holding his own." Silence finally descended and as the door opened, the warrior, my hero stood holding by its leg the now deceased freak of nature. "Aye that were a bit of a beastie lad."

It may have been the adrenalin rushing through my veins, or the fear of meeting another of the spider's family but I was able to install both the table and seat in record time. As I stood proudly back to admire my accomplishment hands on hips, basking in the glory. I was joined by my wife who boosted my ego by agreeing that I had actually done a fantastic job. She handed me a rewarding cup of coffee which I place on my new flip down two seater table with not so much as a hint of movement, as I slipped into the seat... my new personally designed Daddy seat with a sigh of absolute contentment there I remained all day dreaming of the fun I would have with Nan until night stole the ability to see any longer.

THE BANSHEE OF LAKE BALA

I have just had a domestic with the wife over the credit card bill; I keep trying to tell her that it is a limit and not a target. With this in mind I am taking off the shackles of being a restrained gentleman and while I promised the wife that the details of the first night in our campervan would not appear here, I feel there is now some justification to post this.

As you know our first trip was over to Lake Bala, and I wish to grovel for your forgiveness in forgetting to tell you that there were In fact four of us on that. There were me, my wife and our two full grown Bull Mastiffs; Gorgeous George and Haribo Harry.

After we had set up on the site and both my wife and I had taken a shower, then having changed our underwear we walked the dogs that seem to have recovered from the traumatic journey far quicker than us. We settled down for the evening in Nan our dear old campervan and I would like to think she was enjoying the outing as much as us.

I have warm images of her telling all the nearby caravans and campervans "I am thirty four years old you know" and also had visions of her taking on the role of a gypsy fortune teller and scaring the brand new motor home parked next to us by telling it that within three years it would be taken to a place where poorly cars sit and a human with oily hands would take great delight in shoving a rod up its exhaust pipe...I say this, as it is the only reason I can think of why it hurriedly packed up and left.

We set out the beds; the dogs were on theirs in a flash and asleep in seconds. My wife with all the grace of orang-utan climbed up into the over-cab bed and I would like to say I did similar but she assures me there was no grace in my red faced effort to join her but finally I did. I am told Nan may once have had a set of ladders but they have long since disappeared...and were soon to be sorely missed.

As we snuggled down on our memory foam mattress, my wife turned to face me and as I looked into her beautiful big blue eyes...I am putting it down to poor light...but the look I mistakenly saw was the 'come here big boy' look and not the 'you nearly killed me, and now you're going to pay for it' look. In such a sweet voice she told me to hold onto the duvet and as I grabbed our Tesco No Frills five tog duvet in our Tesco No Frills duvet cover (specially bought for this outing) it suddenly started to flap round like a flag in a storm and even now I can only describe the sound that escaped from underneath as a screeching screaming banshee.

As I looked at her in surprise, George having been jolted awake let off one of his trademark not-so-silent-but-deadlies, Harry not wanting to be left out joined in with a good imitation of a machine gun. Now Nan is only a small camper and soon filled up with obnoxious gases. In panic I tried to open the sky-light above my head only to find it had been sealed shut. Vaguely remembering from my school chemistry lessons that methane was highly flammable in enclosed space, I found I had an unbelievable urge to set it free. Now finding myself stuck in the overhead cab five feet off the ground and sorely in need of the missing ladders I realised I had to be the hero and instead of lowering myself belly down and dropping, I went with the more manly (or stupid) technique of lowering myself down using my bottom and arms, with my muscles giving out, my arms started to shake trying to cope with my fifteen stone weight I quickly realised my mistake.

It is at this point Nan having taking offence at what was going on inside her grabbed/hooked onto the back of my boxer shorts these were not just any boxer shorts...these were brand new M&S boxer shorts! As my arms finally gave way, the Nan induced wedgie started to really burn. My M&S boxer shorts quickly became an M&S Lady thong. I was stuck in the middle of a tug of war between my now M&S Lady thong and gravity. Gravity finally winning, with what was left of my underwear hanging like a trophy, depositing me on the floor naked and in pain, getting up I raced to open the other sky-light and side sliding window, only just stopping myself from flinging open the back door for fear of mentally scarring other campers.

I am not going to lie, but the cold breeze felt REAL good around my injured parts...but still the smells lingered.... I shot through to the cab running the risk of being impaled on the gearstick then the hand brake, seat belt holders and arm rests, in the end managing to roll down the windows while leaving the windscreen curtains closed. In the mean time my wife having laughed so hysterically had had what we call a Tena Lady moment and had hidden herself in the toilet.

As the cold started to bite I was just in the process of climbing back up into the over-cab bed this time belly down, I pulled myself onto my knees just as the wife exited the toilet and while I could not see her face her dulcet northern tones announced for all to hear ... "Good people of Bala...tonight...there will be two moons."

REPERCUSSIONS OF BALA

'Payback's a bitch' In our home, this is one of the more frequently used sayings. Our relationship thrives on constant one-upmanship and is sometimes more like a battle of the sexes. I must admit to gloating somewhat over the knockout blow of me recounting her banshee fart of Bala, to a book which will be read by thousands!

It seems that I only won a battle, not the war, the gloves have now come off...and I am sorry to say, she has now competitively dropped her lady like demure, on most days she is now more vocal with her derriere than her mouth, and that let me tell you, is some feat. There are some times as I watch her mouth flapping up and down droning on and on and on. As I faze out I find myself oblivious to what she is saying, in my mind her voice starts to sound like the teacher from that 80's TV cartoon Snoopy silently musing at how she manages to go so long without taking a breath...I'm sure that all the men will be nodding in agreement here and all the women will be watching to see if they do... Sometimes the compulsion to yell "Breath ... God damn it woman... BREATH!!!" overcomes me.

Being the competitive man that I am, I have been plotting away to keep my crown. But first let me tell you, just how I earned the crown in the first place. Imagine the setting, our brand new luxurious multi-functional steam shower with tropical rain head, directional jets, mood setting lights, a radio, a CD player, a panic alarm button and a control panel to rival the star ship USS Enterprise all in an enclosed cubicle pod. But seriously who could you possibly want to make a telephone call to while you are in a shower?? My intentions of having one large enough to shower together (nudge-nudge, wink-wink, say no more) have rather disappointingly been misinterpreted by my wife as a purely water saving, energy economical investment.

There we were clinched in a loving embrace as we playfully tried to hold each other under the shower's tropical storm downpour of water. My buttocks clenched tight as I tried desperately to 'hold one in' for fear of ruining the moment...which was in my mind's eye, like a scene from a Herbal Essence advert. Our childish antics caused the soap to get knocked off the shelf, as I bent to retrieve it the tiniest bird breath of wind escaped. Relieved that my wife hadn't seemed to notice, all was well... Unfortunately heat expands gas and pretty soon the bird's breath became...what I can only describe as an overwhelming mix of rancid eagle halitosis and fermenting rotten eggs. The steam turned to cloudy green fog. There was a desperate struggle as I tried to push open the doors, when in fact you have to slide them, while at the same time trying to hold up my barely conscious wife to prevent her from drowning under the deluge of water. As we stumbled out we must have looked like newly caught fish, wet and floundering, as we gasped in the fresh air as she looked me dead in the eye, I feared her last words to me were going to be "You are a disgusting @$$#%!£ "

Anyhow getting back to the point...so far the best idea I had come up with, was to use a numbing agent, and insert a cork while she slept. But images of her bending over to fuss one dog and accidently shooting the other or even worse me has changed my mind. But with steely determination my mind set on victory, eventually I hatched a 'very very very cunning plan'. As her birthday approached we decided to invite a few friends around to celebrate, our parties are those with soft background music, buffet and drink...lots of drink. As we are all friends we tend to break up into small groups all over the house with us the hosts circulating from group to group...all very laid back. Then at a set time we gather together, for the traditional cake and candles, the Happy Birthday sing-a-long, then to a speech and the giving of presents.

As the morning of the party arrived I put my plan into action, waking up I held back my morning duvet bellow that announces to the world that I am still alive. Normally that loud the wife hears it from downstairs and knows to bring a coffee and my day starts. For the rest of the day I held it all in, ignoring the pain from trying to avoid the chance of any escaping, I ended up walking like a penguin, with my belly bubbling like a witch's cauldron. The people started arriving and the party was soon in full swing, food was consumed and drinks were flowing. But by 8pm I was holding on to the work surface in agony (wondering if it was possible to explode).

Finally my time had come, and as I moved to the centre of the kitchen, heads turned and eyes followed me in the expectation of a speech. As I neared the middle I pretend to walk into an invisible table...with a look of mock surprise and dramatics that were deserving of an Oscar I mimed pulling it across the room, my bottom accompanying me with some awesome sound effects... I WAS BRILIANT!!!! Everyone started giggling...turning with glee, to look where I was expecting to see my wife, bright red with embarrassment and shame. To my utter astonishment I found she was not red at all...in fact she merely raised one perfectly manicured eyebrow, on her completely calm face...with a smirk slowly forming, and a twinkle in her eye........she glided over to my invisible table, and proceeded to pull it all the way back ....better mimes...better sounds. "Actually, I preferred it over here, David!" she declared. The room erupted with laughter. Thinking quickly I grabbed the imaginary table and once again adding the necessary sounds dragged it back. "I want it HERE!". She was having none of it and with even more aggressive sounds pulled it back over "Nope, it is staying here, now leave it ALONE!".

Our friends were now falling around with hysterics, our table-tug-of-war had a couple of ladies running for the loo, and sensing defeat, my concentration slipped and the battle was lost as I emitted a final noise, similar to that of a balloon deflating. My wife walked over to her seat, and looking back and gave me that smile, which puts me firmly in my place with a little shake of her head and a tut that says 'you're sooo cute when you try'. Thoughts flash though my mind...puzzled (how had she known). Fear - did my hero of a wife have real super powers? Could she read minds? Paranoid - did I speak in my sleep? Later that night as we settled down I asked her how she had known "Dave, you wouldn't understand, it's a woman thing ... I know what you are going to do, before you even think about it".

TEMPLE OF DOOM

I in no way intend to upset or offend anyone but I tell you my woes for three reasons the first to warn wannabe/new motor homers (moho's) of the perilous pitfalls they face...the second is to show the hardened moho's how far they have progressed and how much they have forgotten and the third to any campsite owners with the hope that they learn the mental torture that can be caused by ill planning.

I guess before I start my tale of woe I should reconfirm the description of myself...I am a forty three year old 13.5 stone OK! OK! 14.5 stone...fine have it your own way...15 stone truck driver. I am also equipped as is every truck driver with a slight belly bulge...fine...a spare tyre, also recently started to grow a beard (to cover my double chin). Now with me in mind it will help you picture the disaster which befell me.

A few weeks ago we stayed at a popular campsite near Matlock. I say popular as after we had set up I noticed the campsite toilets were busier than the M1 on a Friday afternoon with that certain dread I knew I would need to go. I waited patiently for a break in the constant stream of traffic and I like to think, I walked to the block in a calm and casual "I'm only going for a shower sort of way". However with a northern snort of derision my wife informs me how wrong I was and that it was more like a very camp combination of male fairy, Quasimodo and finally John Cleese (Monty Python) sort of funny walk going on.

16

Any way my luck held and as I entered (what I now call the Temple of Doom) I found an empty stall. After I finished what I had gone in to do, I looked round for the toilet roll dispenser...I looked left, I looked right and only by being able to do what only comes naturally to owls did I finally find it behind me and slightly to the right. As I went through the stages of shock; First - how did I miss that??? Oh yes I was in a rush. Then anger!!! Which flappy-eared webbed footed idiot decided to put it there. Then finally - woe is me!!! Why would they do this to me – what had I done so wrong?

So with a grunt of determination I flapped round and I don't know if it is just me but I tend to hold my breath under exertion and as I started to lose consciousness I finally managed to grab the millimetre of toilet paper poking out. I swung back round to face the door tightly gripping my trophy as my eyes focused on what was in my hand my mind brought forward the advert off the TV. You know the one... "It is I wh-one sheeeet, strong able – wring able". I don't know if it is because I have a big TV or they use some kind of magic in TV land or maybe 'wh-one sheet's' hands were very small but his sheet was considerable larger than the poor excuse of a sheet I now held in my hand.

I don't have Mattel tattooed on my back nor do I answer to the name Barbie!!! I am a fifteen stone hairy bummed trucker called Dave this one sheet was just not going to cut it. By now my jeans had wrapped themselves around my heavy duty steel-toe capped hiking boots which had in turn pinned my ankles to the bottom of the bowl I had also been there that long I had lost feeling in anything lower than my belly button. It's here I feel I lost all self respect and felt my dignity would be also leaving soon.

So like a kitten on a sloped conservatory glass roof I flailed with paws and claws and a wind-milling tail and finally grabbed a doorstep wedge of paper. It is at this point I become aware of other people in this temple of doom and I hoped that the loud noises/grunts/growls I had been making had not left them thinking that

1) I was wrestling a dead salmon
2) playing Twister in the stall....but was in fact
3) trying to reach the toilet roll a usually simple procedure.

As I left the temple of doom my head hung low, my shame clear for all to see and point out I made my way back to my van (called Nan) and still to this day I wonder how such a simple task could go so horribly wrong.

Now has this happened to anyone else or have I just severely embarrassed myself? What Numpty would decide;
1) to put a toilet paper dispenser behind the seat and
2) why oh why just Wh-one sheet? (where was I when this was decided?)
3) For me it's the doggies double quilted all the way...just like I have at home...and now that I think about it why did you all not warn me?

THE BULL MASTIFFS THE WITCH AND BUXTON

Well the painful memories of Bala faded and with a long weekend off work, the weather forecast looked great and the urge to roam these green and pleasant lands again descended upon us...well me anyway. Once again I bravely rose to the challenge of coaxing out the mad old battleaxe for an adventure in Nan as we were now hardened moho's and us Yorkshire folk are a hardy breed...or dumb ass!

Crawling on hands and knees to my wife (I am told this is the standard way to safely approach a Yorkshire woman) once again the road atlas came out and this time the wife's claw poked at the Peak District... hills valleys and narrow roads galore...Yip Yip! Gulp - big smiles all round as we loaded our necessities into the lovely Nan. Throwing in a couple of raw steaks we enticed George and Harry our two large Bull Mastiffs to join us. The sun was out, the birds were singing as we toddled off once again...BUXTON!!! Here we come!!!

As I have mentioned before Nan doesn't start off the key but has numerous buttons and switches that have to be played with in the right order to get her going (just like a woman) however (just like a man) I had forgotten the sequence and after many minutes of fondling, tweaking and flicking she eventually purred to life with more gusto than the wife ever has. Feeling more confident this time as I entered the dual carriage way, I pushed the pedal to the metal and in my mind we took off like a pigeon tied to a lit bonfire rocket!!! However the old dear on a mobility scooter that stayed alongside us told a different story.

As the speedo quivered up to a staggering 50mph, the noise from the engine bay sounded like two skeletons doing something very rude on a tin roof. With my hands stuck in a death grip on her steering wheel, my eyes unable to blink and floods of sweat developing on my forehead, we were on our way to FREEDOM!!!! We were less than ten minutes from home and Nan was already flirting her ponderous backside at any old passing truck, our Garmin Death wish 2000 decided today's first torture would be Derby city centre.

As I looked across to give the wife a reassuring 'I got this' smile, my usually fearsome dragon looked more like a rabbit caught in headlights, her face white as a sheet clinging on to her seat, muttering the words from that famous Englebert Humperdinck song "Please release me...Let me go.....I don't want to be here annnymoooooore". Little did we know her singing would come back to haunt us. As the traffic built up so did my desire to live and the good people of Derby showed great survival skills, most of them managing to mount the kerb to avoid us. I would also like to take this moment to apologise for my five minute nervous breakdown on Friar Gate where Nan decided to play hide and seek with all the gears, leaving us floundering in the middle of the main road out of Derby. I have had to Google some of the colourful words the other frustrated drivers were using and as my mother always said 'you learn something new every day'. Eventually after waving the gear stick round like Paul Daniels and his wand, I found the correct slot. Now there was no stopping us...literally no stopping and luck was truly with us as we sailed across Markeaton roundabout completely unharmed, the faces of other road users squashed against their windscreens will haunt me forever. Although a part of me would like to think they were all rubbernecking to get a good look at the now famous Nan! At this point my bottom actually grabbed hold of one of the buttons of the swish leatherette seats, never in all my twenty nine plus years of driving have I ever had to talk my bottom into letting go of a seat.

We entered the country roads and settled down to a mile eating 30mph, as the views improved the tension ebbed away, I was starting to relax and enjoy the journey. Nan was bravely puffing and wheezing with her skirts up round her thighs as she climbed up and down dale, when suddenly the wife spoke for the first time in hours "I see dead people" confused somewhat, I requested an explanation. "It may be us if you don't find somewhere to pull over, there is about three miles of tailbacks behind us, and a very murderous looking Audi driver attached to our bumper". I dutifully pulled into the next available lay-by (anything to please the one that must be obeyed) and slid slowly beneath the steering wheel, as a very long line of angry people drove past, we surmised they had been there since leaving Derby.

Twenty minutes later and like a Peeping Tom I watched the last car go by before pulling back out and continuing on I pulled out behind a tractor. Oh glory be, what luck! With a guilty puppy like look at my wife I gave in to my herding instinct, and followed the adage safety in numbers... But not for long, blow me have you ever seen how fast some of those new bloody tractors can shift the blooming thing left us for dead.

As we topped a rise, the glorious sun drenched Derbyshire Dales came into view, our satnav said there was only ½ mile to go. How excited was I...a fantastic straight road ahead and I begged Nan to go fast, faster well bless her soul she actually managed a death defying 56mph!!! With the wind whistling through my hair I was in my element, nothing could bring me down... "Oh!!" "Oh?" I replied "Oh dear.. look!" I followed her beady stare over to the passenger side window It was here the wife's earlier singing had summoned up what I can only describe as demonic clouds from deepest darkest hell, racing at full speed towards us.

As we pulled onto the Duke of York campsite, the lady warden was throwing aside her gardening implements in disgust and pulling on waterproofs. She waded across to meet us, we paid our money and moved down to the pitch number fourteen where apparently, the views were amazing, however with tidal waves hitting the windows, gale force winds rocking poor Nan and us clinging to anything secure inside it was hard to tell. I don't know if I lost the will to live or if it was the stress of the moment but it was completely out of character as I turned to my wife of eight years and for the first time ever I grew a pair of balls, telling her that she WOULD keep smiling, she WOULD enjoy this holiday, SHE had wanted to come here, SHE had sung and it was all HER fault!

I had never before been this brave, nor after having come back round will I ever be again...! What a great time to find out I hadn't brought a coat...so my ever prepared wife pulled on her waterproofs and wrestled the door open. And she was right...it is ever so entertaining watching someone trying to fathom how to attach the hook-up cable especially in a storm, but what is more hilarious is watching your wife of 5ft nothing fly past the camper main window followed closely by two bewildered looking Bull Mastiffs. However it is not wise to let her see you on the floor howling in stitches as she fights with the door, dogs on their retractable leads and Nan's rear step to get back in (I actually have a photo, but not the nerve to include it!)

To make it up to my wife for my un-David like behaviour, I saw on the satnav a fish and chip shop only a few miles away, which I thought would be a nice treat. What the Death wish 2000 didn't show were the cliff edges, hairpins, precipices and slaloms, but with intrepid Yorkshire grit, a bum like a rabbits nose, a lot of bitching and moaning from Nan and we made it there and back to the site ...

Now we had been informed that people from this part of Derbyshire are well known for having 6 fingers and the odour of cabbage, as of yet I have not been able to confirm this. Most people we met were helpful and friendly. So there we sat with lukewarm fish and chips, a glass of wine, a candle on the table, and even with 2 pairs of big brown eyes and puddles of shoelace like drool sloshing around our feet a more romantic meal was never had. All tucked up...and I would like to say in that macho way, that it was me that had the van a-rocking but unfortunately if you had come a-knocking, all you would of seen, was me gripping for dear life 5ft off the ground and employing my new found buttock clenching skills to hold onto the mattress piping while a very persistent Nan was bucking in the wind and rain.

The night passed and so did the next day with us hiding out in Nan. As a final treat we decided to risk taking the dogs to the pub for Sunday lunch before setting off for home. The man greeted us warmly, welcoming us and our kids...REALLY....come on I know I am ugly but the dogs as our kids was uncalled for, we found all this rather odd - but when in Rome...or Derbyshire and all that

We settled down in a corner of the pub as this was the first time we had ever taken the dogs in a pub. While we know them well, you can never be sure...both me and the wife were a little nervous. As it turned out they were as good as gold however a flappy-eared southern shandy drinking Evil Edna (I dare you...nay, nay, I double dare you to say that out aloud) accompanied by her troll like offspring appeared and proceeded to spoil the ambience by firing out snotty barbed comments loudly to her family...she was clearly not happy with; the setting, the staff, her holiday, other road users, the weather, her husband, the kids, and certainly not with the odd couple that had had the cheek to bring huge clearly dangerous dogs to where she was about to enjoy a delightful Sunday dinner.

As we got up to leave Gorgeous George stole the show by doing what I can only describe as a dog bottoms version of Rule Britannia. As Evil Edna looked at us with disgust (by this time we were moving quickly to the exit, away from the odour we have experienced many times before) I smiled sweetly at her knowing what was coming next and said "ENJOY". Now I would like to say we sauntered back to Nan but I have to be honest, with sides hurting, eyes watering from laughing at the mayhem unfolding in the pub from George's gracious gift we had to keep stopping to compose ourselves and to an onlooker it must have seemed as if we were three sheets to the wind.

Glad to say the trip home was uneventful for which we are truly grateful.

.

THE LENGTHS YOU GO TO,
TO SAVE MONEY

No camping last weekend due to wife having to work. Ggrrrr! We both have full time jobs to help realise the dream of having a croft in the Highlands, the views, the life style and the lack of people. Everything we do is with the hope of getting this dream to come true, but things like life have a bad habit of getting in the way, so with luck the house will go on the market next year, and a new dream/life will begin.

It's late Friday night and the wife will be home soon, so for a bit of entertainment and wanting to show her how much I love and miss her I set the shower from the tropical rain shower head to the massage jets that face the doors... Oh, and set the temp to freezing (my girl is worth it). Then racing back to bed and pretend I am asleep. Sure enough at 11pm she comes though the door...dumps her bag down, thumps up the stairs and into the bathroom, banging the door shut behind her. Now being together for so long I know she will strip naked, turn the shower on, then as it warms up, she will go for a pee. Having aimed the eight jets to hit different parts of her body and face with the force of a fireman's hose it should be some show. Yep there she goes. Wow can she swear!!! Going to have to Google some of those words!!! Creeping down to the kitchen like a Ninja in M&S boxers, I turn the hot tap on...yep...there she goes again...oh boy...the fun never ends, aren't I a meanie? As I get back into bed and soothed by her screams I soon fall asleep and my snoring resonates around the house.

In the morning I awaken and finding the wife still asleep next to me I slowly sit up and as my derriere gets level with her nose I let out my morning duvet bellow. Now guys, I don't know if you have also been worrying about the tut that ends your morning duvet bellow like I was, but I have since found out, that it is not me but is in fact the wife that tuts!!! Who knew....? (Glad I spoke to the Doctor over that one, it was getting me very worried).

The wife now awake, gets up, makes coffee, lets the dogs out and gets her to-do-list out and as Nan hadn't moved in a few weeks I thought we could take her for a trip out and charge the batteries at the same time. Going into the bathroom to do my daily ablutions and amongst other things, to trim my beard. Unbeknown to me my wife had callously adjusted the head of my shaver, while leaving the setting at my usual six but pushing the razor guard down to 0.5. Unaware that I had been sabotaged I started at my chin, then my right jaw line. However once I noticed the large amount of hair falling to the floor, I rushed to the sink and looking at the mirror, I apparently screamed like a little girl for several minutes while seeing the reflection of the old guy with half a beard and a double chin that was now as bald as a baby's bum. I was only just drowned out by the howls of laughter coming from my wife as she rushed passed me to get to the downstairs toilet.

The first job on the list was to load up Nan with things we no longer need to be taken to the tip. Like I said, we are hoping to downsize if we ever get to the Highlands so we have a lot to get rid of. Sporting my new baby's bum look we left the house. As we drove into the tip, the dedicated Mr Jobs-worth, you know the ones, no teeth and a dingy hi-vis vest tied together with string, came racing over as though the hounds of hell were chasing him. Winding down my keep-fit window to hear him wheeze "no vans...no vans!" while waving his hands in a 'back up' motion.

These people really get my back up, so jumping out of Nan, to show I wasn't going anywhere. I pointed out that this was a campervan. He was having none of it, "it's still a van mate." Really?...*mate*! Run into my fist *mate*! More than once would be great *mate*!!! Pointing to the sign at the entrance, I read out aloud that it states, 'No commercial vans' indignantly adding that Nan hardly provided an income...far from it, and as we were using her to dispose of our own household waste, I couldn't see what his problem was. Well he was adamant I wasn't taking our 'van' in.

Getting back in Nan and contemplating driving over him, I was fuming. "The flappy-eared, flat-footed, jumped-up little despot". Hearing my wife snort, I looked at her in disgust, she was actually laughing...at ME! Apparently I also look like a care bear with tummy ache when I argue. Still giggling, she said "my turn?" I started to feel a little sorry for this guy, as she got out and walked over to him. (Oh boy is he gunna git a whoopin) but no she pulled a piece of paper out of her back pocket, he had a quick look, nodded and stood aside. Climbing back in Nan with a really smug grin, she declared that with hindsight she had already researched the tip regulations and registered Nan as our vehicle with the council office, earlier. So with me flinging items in bins quicker than greased lightening in a strop, we were done. My wife waved sweetly at 'flappy-ears' as we drove out, and we were on to the next item on our agenda.

Our next job is to go get a new mattress for us and give our old one up to our recently moved back home, daughter; you know the type, always get their braces caught on the front door as they leave home for good. Then twang!! Back they fly? Now she is all in with this new technology of Facebook, Twitter and Snapchat and all that. She is never far from her phone and pretty much lives her life on it. To me it's like she was when she was a teenager, only getting a grunt or tut out of her. The only thing that's changed is, there is now a phone stuck to her nose, and to talk to her or if I want to know what she's up to, I have to go on Facebook rather than talk to her across the table!

I remember when a quick phone call use to take five minutes just to put the number in and that was if you didn't put a number in wrong. Did I get old? What happened to the art of conversation? Are Discos just full of people not dancing, just stood there with phones in front of them? How can people live like this?

Oh, by the way if you like watching zombie films and want to know what it would be like to be in one, load up a packed lunch and take a drive down to your nearest university, wait till classes are over and within moments you will have an apocalypse of student zombies with their dead-eyed faces crouched over phones.

My average chat with my daughter goes like this, she never taking her eyes or fingers off the phone. I start with an easy one "Hi babes, how was your day?"
"tut" checking her Facebook page "tut" means Natalie is happy – smiley emoji. I don't give up, I try "how was work?" nothing but a sigh, back to the laptop. Natalie hates working – sad emoji. I give up and close the laptop and go put the kettle on for a coffee, like an idiot while waiting for the kettle to boil I ask "what are you doing tonight?"...she replies
"Huh?" What the bloody hell does "Huh?" mean? Me...racing back to the laptop, opening it...logging on to Facebook...Natalie is meeting Deano – love heart emoji , kissy, kissy emoji, sloppy sloppy emoji... there is also one with a cat and a chicken but I refuse to understand that one! (Note to self...add a whisky to my coffee from now on when talking to daughter). Oh someone just commented on my Facebook page...then out of nowhere "God Dad you are always on that thing, we never get to talk anymore!" then she flounces out the room with me but-but-butting to the now empty room.

Anyway I digress...back to the mattress, having rung our local bed shop earlier in the week and being told he carried stock, we just needed to tell him which one, pay for it and for a small charge he would deliver it for us. However £30 for a five mile round trip is not a small charge. Now being from Yorkshire and with a perfectly good Nan sat on the drive, it was a no brainer; I mean how hard could it be? We set off in Nan a second time, now to get out of our village to the A52 there is a steep hill and if Nan gets a good run up, she can get to the top doing a respectable 15mph. But if for any reason we have to stop, Nan can only get up the hill at 4mph at best and no faster no matter how much I lean forward or push the steering wheel.

I have also heard tell, you all have stereos in your mohos and their engines are so quiet you can hear a pin drop. Well here in Nan we wouldn't even hear the grenade going off that the pin came from, and the only music we get to listen to is Nan's engine's greatest hits of heavy metal thrash. Pulling up outside the bed shop, turning Nan off we went in and picked the mattress we wanted, one of those good old heavy types, and in the sale to boot. As I paid for it I asked the assistant if I could have some help getting the mattress into Nan, with a confused look at me, then my wife, then back at me. Now with all the opportunities that opening left me, I only replied that Nan was my campervan...and not the lady stood next to me. The relief on his face was a picture and he agreed to get someone to help me.

The thing that came to help me load Nan could well have been the missing link that everyone has been looking for and was very reminiscent of the huge gingerbread man on Shrek II called Mongo, so I shall refer to him as such. As I lifted my end with both hands, back locked and knees slightly shaking edged my way backwards out of the shop. Mongo lifted his end with just a finger and thumb. My wife, to save time, had latched Nan's back door open, put the step down and was now in the passenger seat looking into the back. As I stepped onto Nan's step Mongo who it would seem could not count to two steps started pushing with the power of a steam engine. My feet catching on Nan's bottom ledge and unable to shout for help with a face full of mattress, fell backwards onto the floor and watched in horror as Mongo continued to push the mattress into my man-dangles, with me only able to do an impression of a fish and wave my arms feebly about. Mongo pushed me and the mattress for a further few feet. Mongo having felt some resistance pushed his end down which in turn lifted my end up, but only by a few inches, Mongo set to pushing again, this time catching and pushing my family jewels up towards my ears. Eventually the evil mattress let go of them and slammed into my face using my nose as a brake. I dimly remember Mongo helpfully closing Nan's door and even putting the step back up, before tapping on the back window and dragging his knuckles back into the shop.

Lying pinned under the mattress in agony, I glance round in desperate need of help from my wife, only to find her rocking back and forth in stitches with tears streaming down her cheeks. After a few minutes she gained control of herself and sprang forward. Blinking back the tears from my eyes, I watched helplessly as she climbed through from the cab, then proceeded to kick the mattress out of the way, even when she accidently stood on my hand, she was still my hero! It wasn't until she disappeared from sight and I heard the bang of the toilet door that it dawned on me that freeing me from the evil mattress beast wasn't her priority. Abandoned in my moment of need, I struggled with this Mongo induced calamity alone. I fought wildly in this uneven wrestling match with the king size, superior comfort, three thousand pocket spring, latex memory foam monster of a mattress, kicking and squirming before eventually managing to ooze out and crawl into the safety of Nan's cab all the time hurling a string of profanities. Anyone looking at Nan and seeing her bouncing around would have thought we were testing out said mattress. My wife finally joined me sliding into her seat, avoiding eye contact. We drove home in stony silence.

The next task was to get the mattress out of Nan and into our bedroom, without the aid of Mongo. With me lifting and pushing and my wife lifting and pulling the mattress up the stairs and complaining about trapped feet and breaking nails, after what I had just gone though in Nan I was like Catherine Tate "yea but am I bothered? Yea but am I?" My daughter actually managed to put her phone down long enough to find out what all the commotion was; her helpful tip was to use the handles at the side. My helpful tip was to help her bloody mother! The mattress taking offence at being so roughly manhandled decided it's next victim would be our daughter, as she was attempting to squeeze past the mattress in an effort to joining her mother in the battle of getting it to the top of the stairs, this once solid unbending mass of mattress suddenly bowed and pinned her against the wall and while I admit the sight of my daughter being squashed was amazingly funny and the noises she now emitted were hilarious.

My wife once again overcome with a fit of giggles, lost her grip, the mattress seeing its chance made a bid for freedom, me also now weakened by laughter and in no fit state to stop it, ended up pinned for the second time, this time at the bottom of the stairs under its substantial weight. Suddenly in a fit of rage or embarrassment, my daughter developed Mongo like powers and with amazing strength began dragging the mattress up the stairs, sensing the battle was turning and as I could breathe again I rejoined the affray, within seconds this evil mattress was on at the top of the stairs and within a blink of an eye it was in my bedroom and on my bed frame.

Thinking I had had enough bad luck for a month never mind just one day, I would now crawl in to my new bed and close my eyes and the nasty day would go away....but no, one last job to do and that was to take our old mattress into the daughter's room.

I don't think I have mentioned the cat, not only did my daughter invite herself back home, she brought with her, what I can only describe as a semi-feral, schizophrenic, ferocious heathen beast of the devil, with razor sharp claws and teeth that she has no qualms about using. She lures you into a false sense of security by purring and mewing, all cutely pretending she is so pleased to see you, and in the next instant is a flying, hissing fur-ball of teeth and claws. As I opened the door to my daughter's room, carrying the mattress behind me, the cat launched itself across the carpet attacking my socked feet (no shoes allowed in the house by order of Da Management aka the wife) and I promise you it was pure self defence that my foot connected with the fur ball of death and pure bad luck that the cat and its receding battle meow flew though the open window.

So at the end of the day the cat now won't come anywhere near me, my daughter is now not speaking to me, (not that I had noticed and had to be informed by my wife) and as I lay in my new comfy, comfy bed which I am sure will be awesome once all my lumps, bumps and bruises go down. The wife comes in with the last drink of the day and seeing me wince in pain as I reach for the coffee says in her condescending northern dulcet tones "Awww poor-poor baby, do you need a hug? Do you want to tell me where the bad mattress touched you?" Grimacing in pain and putting on my best American accent I reply "MEDIC!! MEDIC!!....MAN DOWN FROM CUTTING REMARK!!!!"

NANS FIRST WILD CAMPING

Having started a new job I am pleased to say I have lost weight (and no...it's not because my lunch box fell off my lap before you start) and I would like to tell you how much, but I can't as the wife threw the scales out after she and the scales had a heated debate about her weight. However I can tell you my moobs are down a cup size and my spare tyre is down to what I think you women call a muffin top (why do I always get an image of Sloggi maxi pants when I say that?).

Looking down at my toes it was nice to see an old friend again. Anyway as I admired myself and my weight loss in the mirror that we have in the bedroom, clenching my buttocks and fishing for a compliment from my wife, who was sat in bed with her laptop Facebooking as usual... "Look at my buns love....they could crush a walnut!!!" Glancing up and then straight back down she said "I would start with a grape and work your way up to a Walnut if I were you." Yorkshire bluntness by 'eck ya gotta love it.

As it was the Bank Holiday weekend we decided to have another go at this camping lark and see if we could get it right for once. After getting dressed we loaded Nan to get ready to go, then turning on the old 'puter we searched for a site. Now what we didn't know is you campers are very organised, you book your pitches years in advance, and we are sort of the last minute escapers). Yes, you guessed it, every site was;

1) fully booked or
2) wanted a 3 day booking and would not let us book for just the Saturday night.
At last we found a site in the New Forest....but only if we got there by 8pm.....it's 3pm - we can do this, grabbing a dog under each arm we raced to Nan.

All loaded up ready to go...me doing the tickling, flicking, pushing and pulling to get her started. Even with a bit of tongue action I could not get Nan going. She would turn over but would not fire up. Well cut me off at the knees and call me tripod!!! My wife would like me to point out that this is a saying and is not based on any real factual evidence, she further insists I point out, that in real life on cold days I have to tie string round it so I can find it to pee. What was I doing sooo wrong with the women in my life? Deciding Nan would be by far the easier to sort out I lifted the bonnet. Finding nothing to stop her starting, I did however spot that she was peeing water all over the floor. My poor Nan was incontinent! Jumping in the car I raced round to a local motor factor shop and came back with some hardened hose and a thingy-me-bob that turns 12v into 240v.

Sliding underneath Nan with my hardened hose, gripping it with both hands I guided it in but no matter how hard I pushed, Nan would have none of it. The hole was simply too tight, even wetting it with my finger didn't help, harking back to my younger days, I remembered once being told if it was too hard or too tight, you put it in really hot boiling water and it would make the end go soft. This I duly did, screaming in agony, as I held my hardened hose under the scolding water...they were right!!! It did go soft. Sliding back under Nan I push my now floppy hose in, the hole was just big enough to fit. I tighten up the clamp and did the same to the other end, there I was lying flat out on the floor, gasping and wheezing pleased with myself, knowing I had done a really good job on her.

Once refilled and bled of air, I put the choke back in as I had pulled it too hard in desperation. I pushed Nan's button and she screamed into life with an amazing amount of vigour, setting off we raced round to fill up, pulling out of the petrol station having managed to squeeze in a whole £45.73p worth of petrol. Nan drinks like a fish but has the tank the size of a thimble. It was at this point our Garmin Death Wish 2000 took great pleasure in telling us we would never make it to the site by 8pm. While the wife rang to let them know we would not be coming, I had fought too hard to give up, I fiddled with the satnav, determined we were going somewhere, anywhere but back home.

Scrolling around Derbyshire then to the Peak District, aha that should do the trick. Closing in, the satnav showed a lane in the middle of nowhere with what looked like a turning circle at the end. I looked at my wife and declared we would go 'wild camping' I knew she wasn't keen, but she had forgotten to book the Sunday and Monday late shift off from work, not just any work, this is M&S work (she really does work at M&S). I don't know if it was me making puppy eyes or the fact there was no site fee which appealed to the Yorkshireness in her. Seeing me jiggling in my seat enthusiastically, although she was slightly dubious, she finally nodded. Throwing Nan into first gear and shouting FREEDOM!!!, we set off on our adventure, and not just any adventure this was our first wild camping adventure.

Thirty minutes after the satnav said we would be there; we finally turned onto the lane we would spend the night on. The delays were caused by Nan's failing head lights, at one point I even considered asking my wife to walk in front with a candle. Most of the journey after leaving the main roads with street lighting was done at a heart stopping, bum twitching 20mph, with brown trouser moments coming thick and fast. Spot lights have now been added to Nan's Christmas pressie list, along with a T.V, a rev counter, ladders, a heater and after the night of a thousand farts (another story) a bloody fan! I really need to get some over-time in at work.

The lane, and I use that word very loosely, had a steep drop on the left and a four foot high bank to the right. In the pitch black it was quite creepy, the occasional tree we crawled passed would screech down the side of Nan like nails down a chalk board. There was no sign of any other human anywhere, no cars, not a single light, just nothingness. The night sky was clear of clouds and full of stars and it would have been beautiful and romantic had it not been for our minds bringing up every image, of every horror movie we had ever seen. But with the braveness of the Yorkshire or the stupidness of the lemming we continued on.

The silhouette of a burnt out car, loomed into view of Nan's dim head lights. Coming to a stop and getting out to assess the road blocking wreck, it slowly dawned on us that we could not move it. Being a man, I did however try to, just to make sure but as I leaned on it, I realised that I am not superman, in fact the only reward I got was a reminder that I am over forty and I should have clenched harder! We could not go forward and with what was in my mind, an axe wielding murderer behind every bush and the trees eerily whispering warnings of our peril, there was no way we were staying there, the only way to go was backwards.

Now in your new-fangled posh campervans, you would have smiled at each other, shrugged your shoulders, before selecting reverse and with the aid of your night vision reversing camera and your purpose designed mirrors, simply backed up, maybe laughing at how you would never have tried this in your old van! Well guess what, I am in an old van made in the era of Polaroid cameras having to wait five minutes for the instant image to be produced. With wing mirrors which harked back to the time when Dorothy Levitt decided to use her handheld compact to see behind. When ladies wore white starched blouses to accompany gentlemen in their automobiles, air bags were only found on new technology vacuums, and for the more daring cruise control was leaning a brick against the accelerator pedal.

What happened next was what I can only describe as the game show from hell. The star prize was us getting out alive and the booby prize was a Nan ten thousand piece jigsaw puzzle at the bottom of the drop. Like two unwilling contestants, in it to win it, we set about getting Nan to safety, ponderous back end first. My wife peered out of the back into the gloom feebly attempting to give me directions. I, leaning out of the wind down window in an inhuman like position half standing and neck straining, with the kinky drivers arm rest trying to boldly go where no arm rest has gone before. We were doing quite well, but needing a rest, I made the signal to 'take five' and collapsed into the seat. As I lit up a cigarette, I could see in the stick-on rear view mirror wifey had done the same.

The game show from hell took this moment to turn up the heat; unbeknown to us a sheep was asleep at the edge of the bank and having opened its eyes to find my wife's cigarette only inches from its nose, let out a bleating bellow of concern. This in turn, made me jump a mile, not the best idea with only two inches of headroom in the cab of Nan. Shooting out of the cab I was just in time to see my wife let rip with a wicked looking round house right hook (I dare you to say this out loud...nay, nay I triple dare you) hitting the sheep squarely in the face and dropping it like a rock. Racing to my wife's aid I tried to comfort her. Part of me counting down the sheep for the knock out as they do in boxing matches.

"Are you all right love? (ah 1er...ah 2er) It's OK it was just a sheep, (ah 3er...ah 4er) you're fine. (ah 5er...ah 6er) You ok? (ah 7er...ah 8er) How's your claw? I mean hand! (...ah 9er) It's ok I got ya (...You're Outta There!)" As the sheep roused, I watched it get back up on jelly legs and turning tail wobbled off, telling every other sheep in the field about its unwanted physical contact.

Turning back to my wife who was leaning against the side of Nan, head up facing the stars her chest quickly rising and falling...rising and falling....rising and falling.... rising and falling...rise -, huh, what? Where was I? Oh yes, she was flapping "Oh my god. Oh my god ...I killed it...I killed it!" Grabbing her by her hands

"No love, its fine, it's over there with the rest of them, look, it's ok, it's fine." Leading my wife round Nan and opening the passenger door I helped her in, then going round to my side I climbed in and continued the task of saving Nan on my own, the hills of Derbyshire now alive with the sound of disturbed sheep. The last hundred and fifty yards back to the road seemed to take forever ... going back slowly, then forward to realign and then backwards again.

My wife slowly coming out of her shock muttering away with a mix of sympathy and anger. "Aw that poor sheep...ow my hand…I hope it's alright…it shouldn't have made me bloody jump." The last one I wholeheartedly agreed with as I rubbed my egg size lump. Finally making it back to the road we headed home. As I reversed Nan into the safety of our drive, my wife looked at me and asked "You won't put this on one of your postie thingies will you?" With a twinkle in my eye, I replied "No love never!!!"

My wife is still very touchy about that night, but me being the irritating, annoying man I am, find great pleasure in taunting her with Rocky style shadow boxing impressions while singing "Baa Baa Black Sheep, have you any wool...thwack!" I will be lucky if she doesn't cut off my tail with a carving knife me thinks...

WHITCHURCH AND THE THETFORD

I am starting to get the feeling that I have the most amazing bad luck at camping or maybe the pitfalls I find myself in are happening to me purely for your entertainment. Our third trip was one of those last minute affairs. I had just picked up Nan from what I like to think she would call a beauty/massage parlour but we call the grease monkey station. I am sure she enjoyed being pampered groped, greased and squeezed by the young mechanic; she certainly left the garage with more vigour and power.

Unwilling to go through the horror and trauma of getting her back on the drive I wimped out and parking her on the road I went in pretending that I had left her on the road on purpose, announcing we should go on a last minute jaunt. Now I don't know if you are like us but if one of us doesn't make a decision we end up sitting there for hours and getting nowhere. The normal process is me whining and crying...and ending up with and wife telling me what we are going to do.

After finding a campsite near to us, SHROPSHIRE was our destination!! A place one would normally only drive through on the way to anywhere/somewhere else. Our Garmin Death wish 2000 said 8:15pm arrival and oh what a sense of humour it has... We managed to make the site at 9:35pm Nan behaved impeccably and because we had stayed on straight roads she had not had any chance to over work my tired buttock muscles.

The only time panic set in was when we over shot the site entrance by five hundred yards and passed a Welcome to Wales sign. This caused a fair amount of pandemonium as it brought back truly painful memories of the night in Bala, from a previous chapter. I would just like to update you on the injuries I received, I am pleased to report that the cream is working well, my man baubles (in comparison to Christmas baubles they too only seem to get used once a year) have stopped swelling, moved back round to the front and I can now nearly walk in a straight line again.

Now in my minds' eye...I yanked on the handbrake while pulling the steering wheel hard to the right and like those American films Nan spun a perfect one hundred and eighty degrees. However in reality the thirty two point turn and the race back to England was kind of embarrassing and took forever.

Initially making an effort to approach the site quietly we found it to be virtually empty and having the place practically to our selves we pin-balled around in the dark trying to get the best views from our windows. Imagine our horror as we woke the next morning to find ourselves parked next to something I can only describe as a small village on wheels. It was feckin huge!!!! It made poor old Nan look like a dinky toy. It made our old lady seem ridiculously small and rather inadequate, although the wife tells me all the time that size doesn't matter.

The site was wonderfully new and sparkly (the washrooms did actually sparkle) even having its own roadside food van at the end of the drive, serving amazing breakfasts and I have to say the cottage pie was to die for...what a find!

I would like to take this moment to say that as a city-dweller and being a long distance trucker I now realised on this trip that 99% of all the sheep I had ever seen on my travels must have been in fact female. As it was here, on this site for the first time in my forty three years of life, I came face-to-face with a fully developed ram. My jaw dropped, my mouth formed a perfect 'O' and I probably looked slightly dodgy as...with childlike fascination I simply stared...for several more moments traumatising flashbacks of Bala and the M&S lady thong episode raced through my mind.

I returned to the van with cold breakfast and much to the dismay of my wife I struggled to find the words to explain what had taken so long. The rest of the day ...was...oh...so boring!!! On previous trips my anguish at driving Nan the elderly camper van like a crazy old lady on day release from the nursing home with a death wish, has got me out of the many laborious tasks such as; fetching water, washing up, cooking, walking the dogs as well as the emptying of the loo cassette, with my guilt ridden wife taking up the slack.

So back to being amazingly bored...left alone, deserted by the wife and dogs, I found myself being drawn to the enigma that is a Thetford toilet cassette, with the sigh of a condemned man I wandered round the tail end of Nan and lifted her flap, with a couple of tugs at the handle out it flew. OK I'm not entirely sure of what to do next but pretty sure Wifey had mentioned the tipping hole thingy being next to the Lady's loo.

Like John Wayne in a western you know, bow legged and bandy with my six-shooter slung low, and my eyes firmly on my enemy, I set off across the barren landscape. There were three touring caravans and their occupants could obviously see I was a virgin to the task and you could see them race to fill the kettles and with coffees in hand find the best seats to watch the show.

I undid the cap over the bowl and just like me after a long day in my lorry it gushed out a never ending stream. I have got to say for such small cassette it holds an amazing amount. As the last few drops came out, I grew very aware of my audience plastered up against their van windows I was determined nothing would go wrong. Fate being the fickle woman that she is decided this was not going to be the case. I turned on the tap for the rinsing process and grabbed the hose. I can hear you all tittering as I am sure in your mind the hose would be whipping round like a snake but no I had my foot firmly placed on it.

As I bent to get a proper grip on the hose it detached itself from the tap and the pressure of the water hit me in an already sensitive area. I quickly turned off the tap and after re-attaching the pipe, triple-checking it could never come off again, I set about sluicing it clean, at the same time trying to hide my wet crotch. I did the typical manly thing, of giving it a few shakes, remembering the saying 'more than a few shakes and you are playing with it.'

Screwing the lid back on I felt, then heard something rattle within my Thetford cassette. I think it is because I had recently watched Pirates of the Caribbean that unbidden images of Johnny Depp and gold sprang to mind. After unscrewing the cap I started shaking it again with the attempt at getting to the treasure. Having no luck and with frustration setting in I managed to prise open the waste gate and peering deep inside I still could not see anything.

Lifting the Thetford up over my head with the waste gate pointing down, there I was swaying it from side to side, then bouncing it up and down in an effort to get it to release its secret. The Thetford taking offence at being shaken so violently fought back and deposited... what I can only describe as a gruesome hell spawned evil blob. It was like being hit in the face by a cold dead trout...a large wet sludgy dollop of toilet paper was now attached to me...ON ME!!! More importantly ON MY FACE...!

As I leaned forward shaking my head the Thetford finally released its hidden gem with the accuracy of a homing missile a small hard object rolled down my jeans and wedged itself between my buttock cheeks. The caravanning audience finally got their money's worth they were treated to a true grit, John Wayne western-style Red Indian war dance complete with whoops and cries as I frantically waved the Thetford about like a tomahawk while contorting my body trying to remove the offending item from down my pants.

Throwing down the cassette my hands raced to remove the offending pulp of doggies double quilted from my face. Oh the horror the more I wiped the messier it became, disintegrating into my hair, my ears, up my nose and in my beard. As my eyes started to focus through the blur I was able to make out the caravans. In the first I could see two pairs of sock covered feet waving in the window, their owners obviously falling about in hysterics. In the second a lady was wiping snorted coffee stains from inside her window and the in third a man, who I would like to think was calling for a paramedic and not taking pictures on his high quality mobile phone.

Abandoning the loo cassette I stumbled my way into the shower room with the still unknown item working its way further and further down, I unceremoniously disrobed...as I slung my jeans off a small dark brown lump rolled to rest between my feet. Please God tell me in my panic I hadn't lost control of my bowels. Sending an SOS text to my wife who receives them with alarming regularity whenever I am left alone and unsupervised. After eight years she is pretty much unfazed by my antics and well used to coming to my rescue, she soon appeared like a guardian angel with a complete set of toiletries.

As she gathered together my strewn clothes she picked up the small brown object and demanded to know why I had in my possession a conker. More than a little relieved that it was a conker, and I had not actually had an accident in the trouser department, I finished my shower. As I told her I had got it from out of the Thetford, her demur changed like something had suddenly dawned on her and bright red she departed in a flurry. Following her over to the camper I was not going to let this go. SHE knew something!!!

On cross examination she came clean, it must have fallen out of her pocket while she was using the loo earlier... Apparently according to the internet they say that conkers deter spiders. So to save me from any intruding critters and the embarrassment that my girly screams would undoubtedly cause on a quiet child free campsite, she had had the foresight to bring one from home. It would seem that we have had several hidden all over our house for the past year. Cuttingly in her northern dulcet tones she also added that if I had ever vacuumed I would have already known about them.

MILLS AND BOON EAT YOUR HEART OUT

I get the feeling that you all feel that my wife is a poor hard done by woman, who in her right mind should have finished off my suffering with a well conceived accident long ago. Then gone and got herself a better man. I will be the first to agree with you and I will be honest, and say that every day I wake up I am always surprised that this amazing woman is still by my side.

We met eight years ago on Facebook of all places, on a little app called social me, it's where you put a picture up of yourself and others rate you, it's a bit like a cattle market but I was bored. Sure enough people started to rate me but only two bothered to comment on my picture. The picture was of me and my son on a bouncy castle, me looking like I had my son pinned down and was smiling in delight. The comment she put was "why don't you pick on someone your own size?" Thinking that my picture could be misconstrued, I sent this total stranger more pictures which clearly showed my four year old son was more than a match for me and over the next few pictures can be seen clearly kicking my buttocks and pinning me face down in the bouncy castle.

Oh how my mother had howled with laughter as she took these pictures, telling me how it reminded her of how my little sister use to do the exact same thing to me. Anyway mails passed back and forth over the next few days, and then one night while I could not sleep and seeing she was still up we chatted, the whole night passed in a blur. It was awesome. She was funny, witty and intelligent; she even found my attempts at humour funny. I had a great night sat in a freezing front room with only a computer and her words as company. As the night wore on we learned about each other, what we did for a living, how many kids we had and where we wanted to go with our lives. Having had such a great night I wanted to show my appreciation for her staying up all night with me, then having to go to work all day, while running her house and looking after her kids.

As nine o'clock of that morning approached, I was outside the nearest florists; nose pressed against the glass, and had I had a tail it would have been wagging like mad as the owner arrived. Hardly giving the poor woman time to open the door I shot in, and made straight for the roses. Now not wanting to be lame, I didn't want to send this larger than life woman twelve red roses. No, no it had to be a special something that didn't say "I am a silly insecure man who has fallen head over heels in love with your words and your one Facebook picture, be mine!!" I wanted these flowers to say "I had a great time talking to you last night, I think you are amazing and please, please, please keep talking to me". Wow these flowers had a hard job to do. I plumped for twelve pink roses with the hope of them saying "cool ex-Yorkshire man (now living in Nottingham) had a great time. Thank you!" and not scream "MARRY ME!!" Paying for them to be delivered, I left the shop. Even the bus that nearly knocked me over would not have got the smile I was wearing off my face.

Getting back into my home and still in a dream like state, I leaned on the back door, congratulating myself on my awesome detective skills, with the aid of Google I had managed to figure out the address of the nursery school she worked at. Smiling at the image I had in my mind of the look of surprise on her face and her smile lighting up the room, as she sniffed the lovingly chosen bouquet. It's at this moment my over tired mind still running on the copious amounts of coffee I had drank though out the night went into insecure over-drive. It suddenly reminded me, that she was sort of seeing someone, OK he had not moved in and it was only a friendship that had the chance to become more, but would the arrival of my flowers cause an argument? My mind was on a roll, as I shot straight up from leaning on the door and staggered a few steps into the kitchen, it now brought forth her description of him. Nearly seven foot tall, five foot wide, slab of muscle that in his spare time played/taught Rugby. What had I done?!!! Looking down at my feet asking them to take me to the sink, at the same time fighting the sudden urge to wet myself.

Thanking God that there was vinyl flooring instead of carpet. Like a zombie I lurched over and as my hands grabbed on to the stainless steel sink in a death grip. My eyes focused on the horrified look on my reflection in the kitchen window. My mind moved in for the 'coup de grace' as it showed this man my imagination had built up, first taking the roses from her petite hands, then jumping in a car and racing to Nottingham. Pushing in my door, re-arranging my body parts and inserting said roses into a most embarrassing place. Before leaving me to find out just how good my Bupa cover really was. It all got too much and I raced up stairs for the toilet, not sure if I was going to be sick, wet or poo myself. For the next twenty minutes I alternated between getting on my knees with my head down the bowl, to standing up, to suddenly sitting down on the seat. The next two and a half hours were spent either going to the toilet or hiding under my duvet imagining the worst.

Finally getting a grip of myself I had an idea. Racing down the stairs and out of the house, ignoring my stomach's warning that it was soooo not a good idea to be this far away from the loo. I raced to the florists. Setting my own personal best at the two hundred metre sprint. In my rush to open the shop door I tripped on the step, falling to my knees and my face slamming into the counter. Leaning back with both hands gripping the counter I looked up, pleading at the lady that had served me only a few hours before "Stop the flowers.....PLEASE Stop the flowers!". She remembering me as the idiot that had bowled her over in an effort to get into her shop first thing that morning, and looked down at me with that 'oh you poor fool' look you women do so well. Leaning over the counter for a better look at this panicking spectacle of a man she said "I can't me duck". Shaking my head in disbelief. She turned her computer screen round and pointed to it "they've already been delivered" moving her finger across the screen "five minutes ago at 12:05".

I am not sure how I got home or how the cold chips and gravy in paper got next to me. As I came back out of my daze, looking round I found myself sat on the toilet with my trousers around my ankles. The sound that had brought me round was my mobile phone ringing, looking at the number and seeing it was the lady from the north I answered tentatively "Hello...?!" Now part of me was hoping it had all been a bad dream, she had loved the flowers and been happy to receive them and I had gone through all this for nothing. But no ... her Northern dulcet tones announced "Yer dead!" All I can tell you, is it's a good job I was already sat on the loo, my guts changed to slush and while I do not want to go into too much detail....hot lava ... say no more, pebble dash... say no more, dying though my bottom. "Sorry?" I asked, trying to cover the sounds of my world falling apart. "You are so dead; I can't believe you did that to me!! Do you know how embarrassing it was to get flowers delivered, when you work in a nursery at a school, in a small village where everyone knows everybody's business?"

I have since being told, by many of the people of said village, the florist had delivered them just as the lunch bell had rung and she along with the whole school were outside for dinner time. Apparently she was bright red as she rushed back into her class room to put the flowers in water. The story of her getting flowers had raced round the village, and by the time the last bell of the day had gone, everyone and their dog was there to watch, as she had not walked but floated out of the gates, and all the way up the road home with her face matching the bright pink of the roses. Not quite the walk of shame she had made it out to be, I also later found out from her daughter that she really did love the flowers and was seen to smile and go all gooey whenever she looked at them.

Meanwhile back on my toilet, grateful she couldn't see down the phone "I...I...I just thought I had a great time talking to you last night and I wanted to say thank you". Imagine my relief, as she replied "Well they are very nice...maybe we should ...you know ...meet and have a drink?" Just like that I was floating higher than the space station. Play it cool Dave ...play it cool "When?" shot out of me like a bullet out of a barrel. Oh yes... Dave so cool! "I don't know, how about next month?" WHAT? Noooo! No way would I be able to last that length of time, my bravado would be long gone by then! "I don't want to wait that long" I stammered.

"Next week then?"

"I don't want to wait that long" I repeated.

"Well, when are you thinking?" Taking a deep breath and crossing my fingers "erm ... tonight?"

"TONIGHT!?" She almost screamed down the phone. Did I detect a hint of panic in her voice? There was a long pause and I feared she was figuring a way of letting me down gently "OK, sure, what time and where?" In the end we decided to meet up at a pub just off junction thirty eight of the M1 as it was near to where she lived and was easy for me to get to. Oh the practicalities of being in love and from Yorkshire.

The time to meet was set at 7pm, saying our goodbyes and me, trying to be funny said "no no you put the phone down first". Well bugger me she did, just like that. The time was just gone 4pm only three hours till I met this woman in real life. Sorting myself out and getting off the toilet. I put the plug in the bath, started it running and because I still had no feelings in my legs I crawled through to the bedroom to pick out what I would wear to this date. While in the bath I was trying to keep calm and think of funny, witty remarks to keep the chat going though the evening. I set about washing and cleaning myself. By the time I was dressed in my new jeans, tee-shirt and leather jacket it was just gone five. Doing the quick maths of distance, plus traffic jams I decided that if I set off now I would get to the pub at about ten to seven.

Racing to the car and being a bit giddy, in my mind's eye I slide over the bonnet like batman from the 1960s, however I don't remember him picking himself off the floor rubbing his tender rump. Within minutes, I was on the motorway heading north, there had been no crawling to get on and it was clear of rush hour traffic. Soon the car was up to 90mph and the junctions started to fly by, even the radio was playing my type of music, such great hits as Brian Adams 'I am going to run to you', Abracadabra 'I wanna reach out and grab ya' to name but a few. I went past Sheffield's Meadow Hall at 80mph and never had to slow down once. I ended up at the pub an whole hour early, climbing out the car I checked my phone fifty five minutes to go and that was if she was on time and not lady like and fashionably late.

Lighting my tenth cig in as many minutes, I checked my phone and saw her text asking if I had set off. I replied that I had, then received another asking how far I had got. Seconds after I answered telling her I was already at the pub. I jumped a bloody mile when my phone screamed to life. "What do you mean you're at the pub already???" Weakly I replied....
"There was no traffic....no rush hour, I never dropped below eighty all the way up, it's OK I will wait, see you at seven". Her parting words were
"Give me fifteen minutes" and the line went dead, she sounded so angry. Worried I had upset her, I nearly ran to the car and raced for home, but the need to meet this woman was so strong I stayed the course. Now I have been told by her and her daughters, that as soon as she put the phone down from agreeing to meet me for the date she ripped round her house screaming orders for them to help tidy up, while organising their dinners, choosing her clothes, having a bath, doing her make-up and hair and trying to vac and wash-up all at the same time. After the last phone call she yelled at her oldest to watch her sister, she wouldn't be long. As she grabbed her car keys and rushed out the door, driving so fast she would have made Nigel Mansell scream like a baby with fright, she raced off to meet me.

As she got out of the car I realised that cameras do lie, standing just over 5ft tall with a petite figure wearing tight jeans; a white bodice and a loose simmering pink/purple see though shirt, her hair was light brown with blonde high lights and long enough to hang over her shoulders, her eyes were like dark sapphires, to me, she was beautiful. So much so I forgot to breath. There I was with the most beautiful woman in the world and rather than enjoying the moment, I was more concerned that I was having an attack as my heart kept missing a beat, then stopping and finally racing. Now it could been down to a lack of oxygen and possibly a panic attack, but to me she seemed to glide over to where I stood, and on tip toes kissed me straight on the lips ... on our first date no less..... Having completely lost my ability to speak I gestured we should go into the pub, ushering her in first as I was desperately trying to pull myself together.

I headed for the bar, before realising I had no idea what she wanted to drink. As I looked over helplessly she smiled and asked for a white wine with lemonade. I was surprised the bartender didn't ask me for ID as I was as nervous as a schoolboy on his first date. We must have chatted but no matter how hard I try I can only remember thinking I must have sounded like a blithering idiot. She was much prettier than in her photo, I could not get over her eyes, her smile, her everything!!! We decided to take our drinks outside, so we could smoke. I had to keep pinching myself to see if I was dreaming, it didn't seem possible that such a woman would want to be in the same county as me, let alone be sitting opposite to me and wanting to get to know me better and I am not sure if she got fed up of my star struck antics or was starting to relax in my company but she got up from her side of the bench and she moved round to sit next to me, NEXT TO ME!!! Our arms touching no less... (My wife, with her northern snort of derision, has just asked me to point out it was actually because it was rather unnerving having me staring at her across the table with drool hanging off my chin, and she too was fighting the urge to run for her car).

Eventually our drinks were finished and not wanting the night to end I offered to go and get more, she agreed so back to the bar we went, getting served we moved to a small two seat settee. Dear lord our knees were now touching!! She carried on talking and I carried on staring dumbly and trying to nod at the right times after about twenty minutes I started to relax and join in more. With the drinks finally finished again and with us both driving I was sure the night was over. But no, to my shock I was invited back to hers for a coffee. Not trusting the kids to be behaving themselves at home, she was eager to get back, but didn't want to stop getting to know me. Like I was going to say no!!! Mind you let's be honest here, like I would have said anything other than just nod, jumping in my car I followed her to a house in a small village a few miles away, pulling up into her own private car park, she stopping just long enough to tell me to wait at the steps while she went in to see what mess there was inside.

A few minutes later a young girl of about sixteen came out the door, burped in my face then looking me up and down proceeded to walk passed me. She in turn was followed by about half a dozen, adolescent Neanderthals all over six foot tall, glaring at me like I was the devil himself, as they jostled with each other to get out of the house. In alarm I tried to recall how many kids she said she had. I was fairly certain she said two girls and nothing about boys. Glancing at my car and thinking I should make a run for it. Too late! She came to call me in. As I walked in I heard her other girl shout from upstairs "who the **** is that?"

"it's Dave now be nice"

"who the ***k is Dave?" Giggling and laughing as her mum went up to settle her down for the night. Coming back down the stairs, apologising for her children's behaviour and doing that smile I have come to love so much (it's kind of a mix of why me lord and a sad bloodhound).

We spent the next hour chatting away, drinking coffee and admiring the flowers I had sent up. At 10:30pm I very conscious of out staying my welcome and decided I would take my leave, and unwilling moved to the door. Even to this day I have no idea why I started shaking maybe it was the stress of the day, maybe it was the thought of leaving this wonderful woman. All I had to do was make it out the door and no one would ever have known. But as this beautiful creature came over and held me in a goodbye embrace, she noticed how much I was shaking and refused to let me go.... Still to this day she has been true to her word and we have never been apart, well not by choice.

Now while I am the male of the species and though I am the stronger in muscle power than this five foot female. I am the first to freely admit that she, as are most women I have met, are most defiantly the stronger of the species. I am like a broken clock, in that I am right, at best twice a day. While she is right so much more of the time, her strengths are so numerous I can never hope to compete, I lose in determination; staying power, energy, her caring nature, compassion and patience, I always seem to find my limit yet she never does. She may not be perfect but she is to me. I am but a child to her and she watches over me as I play at being an adult. I in return will move heaven and earth to make her smile or laugh.... And after she reads this there will be no living with her.

TROUBLE WITH SHOPPING

Shopping - we all do it, and we all have a different way of doing it. My wife likes to race in, grab what she, the dogs and the fish need, if she remembers and I have been very, very good she will get me something too. If I ever dare to moan about the lack of food in the house she says it's because I am a fussy eater.

No dear, it's because you bought yourself enough food for five days and only got me enough for two days. Here is another thing I don't get, why do they then try to make the food last six or seven days before they go shopping again? It's not that I eat a lot, I only eat once a day and that is normally a sandwich or something quick and easy. After fighting traffic all day and getting my hands dirty from God knows what, I don't like to put food in my mouth until I can get home and have a wash.

I try and stay away from fast foods, the price they charge for a readymade sandwich, to me is day light robbery and especially to a Yorkshire man with a big appetite that needs to have three of them. Don't even look at me like that; it's all I will eat until the next day. Now I don't shop at M&S or Waitrose, in fact my wife has banned me from going into these with her, as I am unable to keep quiet at the price of stuff. She doesn't find it funny when I say in my loud carrying voice "Ooooh look love, this isn't just any loaf of bread it's an overpriced M&S loaf of bread". And anyway I always get the feeling I am buying the same food I would get from a cheaper supermarket brand but am paying more for it because it's in a pretty pack and they have a catchy marketing phrase, 'this isn't just an ordinary grape this is an M&S grape' REALLY??? What's so different about it? £1.25 gets me a large punnet at Tesco but only gets me 8 M&S grapes!

However, that said, the clothes are very well made and after a recent trip to Bala, where I put a pair of M&S boxers though their paces and ultimately their destruction I feel it only fair to say that Asda's George or Tesco's F&F boxers would not have put up such a gallant effort. Oh and the picture of a male pig, yes I had forgotten about that, and probably the main reason I'm not allowed back in...ok so they had a picture of a pig on the wall as part of their display but not just any pig, this was a male pig, with man dangles the size of 1970s space hoppers, and OK I admit I did forget my volume control, as I shouted "Hey love, look at size of those bad boys", while pointing to the pigs Balearics (at this point every other shopper and member of staff also turned to look). "They are fake right? ... He's had a nut job right?" My wife's face was a picture as she glanced round to see everyone staring at us; she threw the cashier a 'please shoot me now' look as she quickly packed up our purchases into bags, head bowed and mumbling about how I was living on borrowed time, and to just wait till she got me home!

I don't like Aldi or Lidl either, as they remind me of Tesco's in the late 70s early 80s - stack it high but with not much choice, and yes while your shopping is cheaper that's only because you didn't get half the things on your list, as they don't sell it. Then when you get to the checkout the cashiers scan it though at the speed of light, on to the tiniest shelf so you have no choice but to dump it into your trolley, only to then, by some unwritten rule, have go over to the side counter looking like a lost bullied child and re-pack it into your bags. I even tried to be smart and had the bags open ready, total waste of time the guy scanning only saw this as a challenge, one I was clearly not up to, and in the end he just pushed the whole shop straight off into the trolley.

That leaves Morrison's, Tesco, Asda, and Sainsbury's out of theses I don't like Asda or Tesco as the food seems to go out of date as soon as I leave the shop that said they have got better but the image remains. So down to the last two, I love both, but Morrison's Market Street is my down fall, the smell is amazing, all that fresh bread, cream cakes and deli meats (one second I am just wiping the drool off my keyboard) I just have to have them all. I find I have over-filled my trolley after the first aisle so I have to go pay, then come back in to do the real shop. To be fair we usually can't eat it all and most of it ends up in the bin or the dogs and the down side is their frozen section is a bit small. Just realised that you Southern shandy drinkers might not have heard of Morrison's as I think they are known as Safeway's down there. My wife loves Morrison's too as it reminds her of home, but the nearest to us is twelve miles away.

So it is to Sainsbury's we will go to do a weekly shop. Now my wife doesn't mind Sainsbury's, but once had a bad experience in the Huddersfield one. Was I there? I hear you ask ...why yes! How did you know? Was I the cause of her bad experience? Why yes, in a way I was! I promise you I never knew it would end like that. Before we moved in together, down here in Nottingham we did that run 2 houses thing, hers in a village just outside Huddersfield. Every morning I would drive to mine in Nottingham, go to work then drive back to hers in the evening. As things were going well and I had the next day off, she had decided that it was time I met her family. She would go easy on me and I would only have to meet her mother and her grandmother.

The morning arrived and we set off in my car to meet my future mother in law. When we first pulled up I had a bit of trouble letting go of the steering wheel but with my wife's DIY skills and a screwdriver, I was soon freed. She led the way and I followed like a lost puppy (on a choke chain), her mother was to be found in the kitchen. I was introduced, eager to make a good impression I leaned over her bubbling cauldron to shake her hand, as she grasped my hand, she said to me "So you're the poor fool that's making her happy are ya?" and just like that we dropped into our roles that have continued to this day. She is the wicked witch of the north and I am the dozy long suffering other half of her daughter.

After a few cups of tea and several trips to the little boys room (Yorkshire water goes straight though me, not enough chemicals in it to slow it down like Nottinghamshire water) we set off the meet the grandmother. Me racing for the car, my wife-to-be telling me not to be silly and opening the front door to a house three doors up from her mother's, she disappeared inside, me muttering under my breath that I am not a mind reader and I don't have crystal balls, took off after her like a scared of losing my mummy school boy .

After quick introductions I was left with Grandma as her granddaughter set to cleaning the house as she did each week. This elderly woman was amazing, while she was frail in body, she was sharp as a razor with her tongue, mind and hearing, within minutes we were laughing and joking as if we had known each other for years. Sadly she is no longer with us and is sorely missed. But I will never forget the words she said to her granddaughter "Listen up Elizabeth, mind you look after this one I reckon he's a gud'en!"
"Aye happen" my wife-to-be replied, grabbing her grandmother's shopping list and pulling on her coat. Making quick goodbyes and was lovely to meets yous, I followed only to be told I could have stayed and she would have caught the bus. Over my dead body there was no way I was going to sit around drinking tea and let her catch a bus into town and then one back loaded with shopping. What kind of man did she think I was? Opening the door to the car and in my best Parker off the Thunderbirds voice "yes mi lady". As she climbed in her mother came out and asked if we were going already telling her we were just going to get the shopping, she asked to join us. Smiling I quipped "the broomstick broken again huh?" Looking me right in the eyes she said "yes ... It's in the garage being repaired, after I wrapped it round the head of the last person that thought he was funny".

Me put firmly back in my place opened the rear door for her like a chauffeur. Arriving at Sainsbury's my wife to be grabbed a basket and shot off to fulfil her grandmother's list. Leaving me and the wicked witch to sort ourselves out, I grabbed a trolley and asked if she would help point out anything her daughter would eat as I had stayed there for over a week and wanted to fill her cupboards back up. So off we went filling the trolley with food, when we got to the aisle of biscuits me still in the role of the poor hard done by boyfriend of her daughter, made a comment about liking a certain biscuit, she told me to get them. Turning to face her in mock horror "I can't ... if I pick the wrong ones she will hurt me", I said "Don't be silly, pick a few different ones then" she replied. Turning back to the biscuits I replied "no no ... if I pick the wrong ones she will make my life a living hell, I will have to go find her and make sure which ones are the right ones", leaving her with the trolley I set off look for my wife-to-be. I passed a very pretty woman (I am to point out that while this woman was very pretty she was nowhere near as pretty as my wife, and that my wife is not looking over my shoulder and forcing me to type this) who had overheard our banter and unbeknown to us must have taken what I had said seriously.

Now this lady started to follow us around the aisles and obviously misconstrued my gentlemanly pushing of the trolley and my eagerness to please as an act of subservience and sufferance and by the time she had watched me pay for all the shopping and carry all the bags, this lady had seen enough and walked up to my soon to be wife under the firm belief that I was a victim of domestic abuse and in a loud voice said "it's disgusting how you treat him", before shaking her head, and leaving the store. My wife to be's face was a picture and if I had suddenly whipped out a cold wet fish and slapped it across her face she would not have looked any more shocked. It was only on the way back to her grandmothers did we finally figure out what had just happened. Pulling up, she stormed off in a huff, but her mother and I were unable to follow as we were laughing so hard we were crying.

I seem to have digressed – I apologise. So back to our weekly shop in Sainsbury's. I have arranged to meet my wife there, she will come from home and I will come from work and yes I will be in my work gear. Grabbing a trolley we set off to do battle, within two minutes I had had my ankles taken out twice, after the first one I said "don't worry love, I got another foot", the second one was daft enough to say "oh I am so sorry, I didn't see you there", my wife hearing this and knowing me so well winced as she knew I was cocking the double-barrel shot gun so to speak "really?" I replied "you must let me know which part of this Day-Glo orange boiler suit you did not see!" and having made my cutting remark I limped off round the corner.

Yes because I recover broken down cars I have to wear a bright orange suit as part of the health and safety code. And I am afraid to say I have had several memos telling me I am not the man out of the Tango adverts and could I please refrain from creeping up behind management and screaming ORANGES!!! Also apparently I am to stop grabbing people by the cheeks, licking their noses and saying … "you've just been Tangoed". Having just finished work, which is a battle of the roads and not having had time to calm down from the stress of driving on our delightful roads when driving a truck seems to attract every idiot. Now I have to walk round a supermarket where they have will let anyone loose with a trolley.

Over the last eight years I have tried to train my wife to walk just in front of me while I push the trolley, this is for two reasons
1) so she can forge a path and
2) I get to see what's she's putting in the trolley and if I disagree I can sneak it back out.
But I am sorry to say I have failed miserably, she is either behind me or has shot off somewhere without a word and I really must fight the urge to put a frickin bell on her. As I stroll down the sweetie aisle I stopped to see which treats I might be able to have for being a good boy. After waiting a few minutes, my wife was nowhere to be seen, so I set of to the end of the aisle in search for her.

As I near the end, a mountain of a woman, not unlike an 80's Russian female shot putter rushed passed and realising she had missed the turning, swung her trolley round like a hammer thrower and rammed it at full speed into my trolley. My trolley in turn shot back and knocked the wind out of me, I couldn't utter a sound, nor could I stop myself from doing a slow nose dive into said trolley. Finding myself face down in my shopping with my hands trapped between the push bar and the metal mesh of the trolley I was stuck. My head and body were heavier than my legs and with my arms trapped I could only wave my legs about in a frog like kick, that had no effect other than to catch the shelves and push me further into the main centre aisle, you know the one that runs the whole length of the supermarket. I then tried to lift my legs as high up as I could and drop them quickly, like a Newton's Cradle with hope my head would pop up. This also failed to set me free, however to the twenty or thirty onlookers it must have looked very funny judging by the laughing and sniggering I could now hear.

Like the trapped animal I had become, I gazed out on my new world from behind the bars of my prison and as I relaxed and tried to get my breath back my eyes sending out a plea for help while my bottom let forth a sigh of surrender...and that's another thing why did you guys over forty five not warn us younger men when we got over forty that our iron vice like grip control of our buttocks would suddenly turn into a limp wristed grip with no warning. And that any pushing, pulling or lifting would have added sound effects and the bonus of red faced embarrassment?

Like the time I had to do a collection from a book shop, the lady showing me to the boxes I was to take, me lifting them up, to what was in my mind, the sound of several large ships leaving a foggy harbour. In complete surprise and horror, I just looked at the woman and before I could engage my brain, "thank the lord it was just wind huh?" Flew out of my mouth. I could not get out of there fast enough. The next day I had to collect from the shop again and as I went in shame faced I overheard the lady from yesterday telling another member of staff "......and then he was gone...". (Laughing) "...Gone with the wind literally" (now howling) and me now having to wait red faced for her to compose herself. And to all the men over forty five laughing at this, also know I have the urge to tell your wife to hit you round the head with a rolled up Woman's weekly for not warning me....

Damn it I digressed again...where was I? Ah yes in the middle of Sainsbury's, head down, bum up in a trolley that was in the main aisle with people pointing, staring and laughing at me. As the trolley is still slowly spinning I catch sight of my wife, on her way back from picking shampoo, stopped dead at the end of the aisle and had then moved back to hide, while she made up her mind whether to walk out the shop and deny all knowledge of knowing me or endure the humiliation of rescuing me. Rolling her eyes, she headed towards me, I can read her thoughts like a book, first she goes though her wedding vows wondering when she agreed to be with this unlucky accident prone man and how much more she must suffer before the death-do-us-part comes into play. Then maybe she could just divorce me on the grounds of mental cruelty. Finally sighing as she tells herself that she really does love me and it's not pity. She pushes me and the trolley up against the chiller of ready to cook chickens and puts her foot against the wheel to stop it rolling away, then starts to push down on my legs, while I try to help by doing a weird sort of wriggle and what looks like a rude humping of the trolley to get up straight.

Finally my feet touch the ground and I was free, looking round for Olga the mountain of a woman, to show my long suffering wife who had been to blame for my entanglement. Both of us now eager to leave we resumed the shopping at break neck speed, my wife hurrying off to get things off the list and issuing orders at me which I shot off to fulfil. On getting back from one of these orders I noticed a new pair of shoes in the trolley. Oh no she's not having another pair (women you are not spiders you do not need that many shoes) so I put them back. My wife sends me on another errand this time I am delayed by the blue rinse brigade who I am of the firm belief are not there to shop but are only there in a ploy hold us up.

In my mind's eye I see a white 'help the aged' mini bus pull up with Mrs Bucket from 'Keeping Up Appearances' in the front passenger seat who turns to Oslo "be a dear go get the Zimmer frames unloaded", then grabbing her clipboard turns to the passengers in the back "now George you are on Ladies underwear...is that the best rain mac you have ?"..."do try to get a longer one for next time dear!"...Lily and Mavis you are on pills and medicine...now remember Mavis it does help if you leave your trolley in the middle of the isle...Lily remember try to look for the haemorrhoid cream with the small print"…"Rose, Gladys, fresh cream and milk aisle...got your thermals?...Good, good...Rose put your hat on straight dear, it's a day out not a singles bar… Ethel, Doris you two on the fresh fruit aisle, now remember ladies I want to see lots of squeezing and prodding!...Miriam you're on eight items or less express checkout...do remember nine items and do remember to look in your basket, so you can pick something that's not already there, it makes you look unstable dear, when you have it already...now chop, chop ladies...and remember double marks for ingenuity...come on...come on" as she herds them into the shop then races for the coffee bar on the first floor to watch and give marks on her clip board.

Anyway I finally make it back to the trolley only to find my wife has put the shoes back in. She never learns! So I take them and put them back on the shelf again. Finally we get to the checkout and with me unloading the trolley onto the conveyer and her packing it into the bags, the torment has nearly ended. As I load the shopping on I come across another pair of shoes, that sneaky low down wife of mine had put two pairs in, one on the top which she knew I would put back and hidden another under all the food. With my best 'I am so angry at you' face I look across at her, she looks back with that 'whatever' smirk knowing she has won, she knows I won't take them back when I am this close to freedom. Having loaded the shopping on I move down to load the full bags back into the trolley, it's at this point my wife lets me know she hasn't got her purse. "...and my wallet is in my car, hang on I'll have to go out for it!" and like a knight in rusty armour I set off to go fetch it.

Getting to the car I leaned in to reach my wallet and as I looked through the windscreen I could see my wife packing the last of the shopping into the bags, seeing her put the shoes she has sneaked into the trolley. I came up with a cunning plan to teach her a lesson! I would not race back to this flappy-eared, concord nosed, low down, sneaky, shoe hiding damsel in distress. Oh no! I would just sit in the car and wait. I lit up a cig and watched as she finished loading the bags up, telling the cashier that her husband won't be long in getting his wallet. Then she loads the remainder of the bags into the trolley. It's at this point I start to see the panic spread across her face as anxiously she looks out for me returning. The cashier has got bored and has started picking her nails. The people waiting behind her are starting to shuffle and give my wife dirty looks.

Well there I was laughing so hard, that hard that I slapped the steering wheel, accidently honking the horn. My wife glanced up to see me sitting in the car with a cig hanging out my and mouth waving back at her. As it dawned on her she had been had, with a furious look spreading across her face, she picked up the crusty white baguette, holding it aloft, and with her steely eyes locked on to mine she ripped it clean in half. This brought me eye wateringly back to my senses and completely forgetting about teaching her a lesson, Boy was she mad! I sprinted back to the checkout with my card, typing in my magic number all the while apologising profusely to the cashier and waiting queue. I dare not even glance at my very, very angry wife. She stormed off, leaving me to load the car alone and when I got home to put all the shopping away in silence, let's just say I spent a long, long time in Coventry over that episode.

IT HAD A NICE RING TO IT

In this next post I thought I would write about another of my traumas of living with this beautiful, hard as nails, blue-eyed, northern lass of mine and my attempts at trying to woo, impress and show her how much she means to me. A three month whirlwind romance found us buying a house, moving in, and starting our new lives together in Nottingham.

As December approached we were determined to make our first Christmas the best, the kids had deserved it. They had been great with the upheaval of coming together as a new family. We were in the fifth month of a huge building project, as I turned our home into a building site. I basically had the whole house taken apart to rewire it, put in central heating, remove walls and cupboards to make rooms bigger and convert an extra bedroom. I was also adding; a conservatory, a downstairs toilet, a porch and a stone fireplace. The bathroom was having a Jacuzzi bath and steam shower. The new kitchen was having granite work tops, an American fridge freezer, dish washer, washing machine, tumble dryer and a range cooker. Having spent a lot of money on the house making sure that the woman of my dreams would want for nothing.

The kids and I were taking it all in our stride and looked on it all as an adventure. My wife on the other hand, being very house proud would follow the builders and other tradesmen around armed with her Dyson, wet cloth, duster and Pledge. The minute they nipped out to fetch something or go to the toilet she would dive into where they had been working and start cleaning it up. They would come back and have to wait till she had finished, then smile politely at her before they un-rearranged their tools. Now throughout that blitz, to me she was wonder woman, she managed to cook, clean, wash by hand, iron and shop for three kids and me. However to the workmen she had become a bit of a nightmare and for the first hour of every day they would make a mess in one room and once my wife shot in with manic glee to clean it, they would then move to another room to actually get some work done. It got to the point that the builders insisted I took her to work with me. My office never looked so clean!!

Anyway back to my tail of woe...because we had spent a bundle on the kids, my wife decided that we weren't going to buy each other a Christmas present. Unhappily I agreed. Unwise in the ways of female thinking, I took this to be law, and all was well in my life, until my eldest daughter let slip that my wife had indeed got me a present. My once happy world was, in that instant turned upside down. I with disbelief learnt the lesson of a woman saying one thing and meaning another!!! And to make matters worse, it was 6pm on Christmas Eve. Racing out of the house with me shouting I had forgotten something at work, I bundled my daughter into the car, and we raced to town. With her running to catch me up I was lucky to find a jeweller that was staying open till 8pm.

I had always thought it rather foolish that men seem to leave their Christmas shopping to the last minute. But as I pushed my way in I was a little grateful for the herd like comradery we now all shared. Did all women do this? Is that why all these men were running round like headless chickens? Were all the women at home enjoying the peace maybe sipping wine and eating mince pies while laughing at us? There were certainly none to be seen running from shop to shop, only daft panic stricken men caught out by our women's wiles.

There I stood looking at the choices of jewellery. First I discounted the necklaces as she had a very pretty one already. Then the ear-rings as she had already lost two pairs since we had met. That left the rings. Now as all men are aware I was entering a mine field here as

the wrong ring would have her racing for the altar. Not wanting to
go down that road yet, I had all wedding like rings removed; still in
this mine field I had all engagement rings removed. I had come to
the conclusion that my Northern Ice Queen would tell me when I
was to propose so I didn't need to panic over them yet.

Eventually I had got my choice down to two, both were pretty but
the one I liked the most was £190.00 more. With the sigh of a
condemned man I plumped for this one. My guts turning to jelly
with all the doubts flashing though my mind, as I tried to think of all
the conceivable things that could go wrong. And as you all know I
have a very over active imagination. With images in my mind of her
going from, looking down her nose and squinting at it, saying "yes
dear it's amazing what you get in crackers nowadays". To her
thinking I was trying to propose and handing it me back demanding a
more romantic scenario. As I calmed myself down and nodded to
the lady, who evidently had better things to do on Christmas Eve,
than wait while I was being tormented by my mind. With a smile like
a cat playing with a mouse, she said "Very nice choice sir ... and do
you know the lady's ring size at all?" Damnit! I had not thought of
that, off I went again. If I got one that was too small, my wife would
think I was telling her she had fat fingers and if it was too big, she
would think I hadn't noticed how elegantly thin her hands were.

There I stood doing an embarrassing, but Oscar winning impression
of a gold fish opening and closing my mouth and flapping my hands.
The lady looking at me with a condescending smirk that yelled 'why
must I always get the Christmas fool?' While some men glancing
sideways gave 'Oh we have a newbie in our mist!' nods. Others gave
me encouraging 'chin up ole boy!' looks. I had no clue to my wife's
ring size; it's not the sort of thing that comes up in conversation. "Hi
my name's Dave, and my ring size is N". That has sort of, to me
anyway, a very camp gay male ring to it (excuse the pun). My
daughter seeing me having a meltdown came to my aid and pointed
out she and her mum often swapped rings (Although I have since
found out this is teenage speak for "I often help myself to my mum's
rings") so if it fitted her it would fit her mum. Great, I was safe to
live another day, turning back to the rings I watched her try them on,
the one I loved was too small!!! The other fitted just right and that

was the one we left the store with, the lady having wrapped the box in Christmas paper and even put a bow on it.

Walking back to the car I thanked my new daughter profusely for saving me from a very embarrassing Christmas morning. That night after the kids went to bed my wife and I put all the presents for the kids under the tree with the exception of one each, that we placed at the bottom of their beds. Then we also turned in for the night, me after that horrible shopping trip slept like the dead and only came round when the kids started calling me from downstairs. Looking round I found my wife had already gone, staggering down the stairs tying my belt round my towelling dressing gown, I entered the kitchen to find every available surface covered in sweets, treats and party food, the dinner table set with festive runners, place mats, candles, glasses and crackers. It all looked amazing. Grabbing a quick coffee I hurried to the front room, our new fire was on, and the golden Christmas tree, with black baubles sitting in the corner looked great with its lights flashing merrily.

The kids were waiting with mounting excitement, each kneeling in a space with their presents in a pile in front of them. Looking over with appreciation at my wife who must have got up so early to work this Christmas miracle, she returned my look with a loving smile. Opening the festivities like another well known jolly fat man with a beard, I declared it was to be a very HAPPY CHRISTMAS!!! Under starter's orders, the kids started ripping wrapping paper off and for over thirty minutes we watched the kid's faces light up with joy and screaming with excitement as each present was revealed. Me and my wife sipped our coffees and took turns opening our own presents from friends and family, stopping every now and then as one of the kids came rushing over to stick a new gift they had received up our noses. It was perfect.

The party moved to the kitchen and we ate a huge dinner, then back into the front room to spend the afternoon watching TV, playing with the new toys and generally having fun and pigging out on the banquet of party food and drink. All too soon it was time for the kids to be collected, each going off to the other respective parents for their next Christmas day. Leaving me and my wife to tidy up and then getting ready for an early night we settled in bed watching TV and relaxing. With no sign of her giving me a present. Maybe my daughter had got it wrong, maybe my wife had kept to her word and had not gotten me anything at all, like she had said in the first place. Ah well! I decided that I would take the ring back and she need never know about it.

However the next morning my wife woke me up with a coffee and as I opened my eyes, there she was holding a present. Oh no!!! Making excuses that I would need the toilet before I opened it. I shot downstairs to grab her present from where I had hidden it, before racing back up and diving into bed. As I offered it to her she seemed flabbergasted. Wanting to know why I had got her a present when she had said not to and that hers to me wasn't much of a present, just something to open really. All the time her fingers proceeded to rip off the wrapping paper (the lady doth protest too much me thinks). Opening the box and seeing the ring she went into jaw-dropping goo mode, all soft and squishy, so out of character for my northern, hard as nails, ice queen. As she put it on, she held it to the light, and then she spun round to let me see it on her finger. We both watched in shock as it slipped directly off and fell onto the bed. It was far too big!!!

My worst nightmare had begun; I looked in horror at her face waiting for the barrage, while bumbling an apology and babbling out the tale of how after agreeing not to get each other presents her daughter had let it slip with "my mum got you one". And how we had raced into town on Christmas Eve to find a present...and how hard it had been at such short notice...and how her daughter had tried it on and said she was sure it would fit...and it had been the best I could do...and I did love her to the moon and back...and again how sorry I was. Begging her not to be cross and to get dressed, I was going sort it.

I took her back to the jewellers; the lady that had originally served me came straight over to my aid, saying it was no big deal to have it cut down to the right size. As she left to get the paper work I asked if she wouldn't mind us looking at the other ring I had really liked on Christmas Eve. She duly came back with it, turning to my wife I told her this was the one I loved, this was the one I wanted to get her, but her daughter had decided it wouldn't have fitted. My wife agreed it was very pretty, yes it was beautiful but she loved that one I had got her. The shop lady gave a fantastic impression of Mrs Doyle; you know the one, the cleaner from Father Ted? "Will you not try it on? You know you want to! ... Go on, go on, go on, go on, GO ON!"

Well bless my soul, and my big cake-hole!!! It fitted like a glove and by the look in my wife's eyes there was no way it was coming back off. The lady of the shop quietly pulling me to one side, offered to swap the rings - if I was happy to pay the difference. Gritting my teeth I handed over my card and we left the shop with me another few pounds lighter. All the way home my wife alternated between gazing at the ring, and smiling at me, then slapping my arm and exclaiming sheepishly that she was so embarrassed as her present wasn't really a present.

When I got home and finally opened her present she was right! There were no keys to a Ferrari, no Rolex watch, no Aran jumper not even boxer shorts, socks or hankies. None of the things I had hinted at possibly wanting for Christmas. Nope, what she actually got ME was a flipping Dunlopillo pillow!!!

WOMEN SHOULD BUGGER OFF BACK TO VENUS!!!

My tale of woe for today's post is from a weekend about six years ago, and I am happy to say it was the last time I ever went to Derby for a clothes shop with my wife. We both decided after that day it would be better for my heath, if I was to never go with her again and to date I am still alive, so it was a good choice my wife made on my behalf.

It all started on a Friday, my eldest daughter then eighteen or nineteen was still living with us but as most teens back then she had found it hard to get a job and with no money coming in, it was decided she would help out by doing chores around the house. I have to be honest and say I feel we were ripped off on that deal. After me going to work, my wife gave her a list of things to do and also told her we would be going out to Pizza Hut that evening when I got home. Now if it were me I would have cleaned the house from top to bottom for a Pizza Hut, but not my daughter, no she goes off into her bedroom and my wife informed me that was the last she saw of her till 5:30 that night. At which point she entered the kitchen, hair all down and recently straightened (my carpets burned yet again where she puts them down forgetting they are still on!!!!), her makeup made up to perfection, her best clothes on and sat there like Lady Muck on her phone.

Getting home at 6pm that evening I opened the door to the house, I was nearly bowled over by my two youngest who having seen me pull up, were racing for the best seats in the car, with my head dizzy from being spun round so fast as the kids had shot passed I had to wonder why they were not like this on the school run. Next came her Royal Highness the eldest, pushing past me, she too went and got in the car, walking into the kitchen I looked at my wife, she was tired but smiling and I am not surprised the house was immaculate. Well that is till I checked the eldest daughters room, that was like a war zone and if I had throw a grenade in it would not have been noticed, it was more untidy now than at the start of the day. It was time to teach my eldest a lesson, it was not fair that my wife and me had worked hard all day and she had just sat in her room getting ready for a free meal having done nothing to earn it. Following my wife out the house and into the car, we set off to Pizza Hut and as we got onto the A52 heading towards Derby, the car having got up to 100mph suddenly developed the weirdest fault.

All four windows suddenly fell down, the two youngest started laughing, the wife having seen me cause the said fault just smiled. The eldest daughter mean while was having a nightmare, trying to hold down her beautifully straightened and lacquered hair from being whistled round by the wind, screaming that she couldn't wind the window up and yelling at the others to stop laughing. By the time we got to the bottom of the A52, she had hair like an 80's pop star and her mascara had merged with her foundation and was smeared down her face from wiping her watering eyes. She looked like the love child of Alice Cooper and Kate Bush. Who would have thought just a few seconds could ruin a full day's hard work? Arriving at Pizza Hut, we were met by a tall six foot tall, broad shouldered, good looking young man, who greeted us with a smile, all polite and chatty as he welcomed and directed us to a table. It then dawned on us he was the reason she had spent so long making herself pretty. Telling him we needed a table for five not four, he did a double-take to re-count the children, he let out a high pitched shriek and recoiled in horror, at the sight of our Rocky Horror Show reject and I am sure he was resisting the urge to make a cross with his fingers to ward off the demon.

Falling back on his extensive Pizza Hut training he quickly recovered and sprinted us over to our table. My eldest disappeared behind a menu, desperately trying to sort herself out. Our orders were taken and our food delivered to our table, the eldest having ordered the biggest and most expensive pizza, garlic bread and a bucket of fries tucked in with vigour. However still fizzing over her lack of help and her free-loading attitude I managed to get in one final cutting remark, when the guy who had seated us asked my eldest where she had "put all that food?" Jumping in I told him, to ask her to stand up and turn round, and you will see where it all went!! My wife looked at me in shock then started laughing; my daughter gave me the evil eye that only a teenager can do, and grinding her teeth and muttering under her breath about how embarrassing I was. Oh she hadn't seen anything yet...I picked up a slice of pepperoni and threw it at her, it landed on her face. Yep I can be really embarrassing! With an "OMG...DAVE!!!!!" she launched it back.

And that was where things started to go wrong. Not to be out done I grabbed a spoon of the ice cream that my wife was eating and flicked it at my eldest, it landed on her neck, she went rigid with shock then scrambled for a serviette to get it off her before it ran down her top. I thought the battle was over but no, a large dollop of ice cream shot passed my ear and landed on the back of the male of a young couple who was having a near face chat with his girlfriend. As the ice cream landed on his back he shot up yelping, his face changing so dramatically that close to his girlfriends face, she in turn fell backwards letting out her own surprised squeal. My daughter looked at me with her hand over her mouth and I looked at her wincing while we waited for all hell to break loose. His reaction was not what we were expecting; it took us by surprise when a tomato flew past my ear, this time going the opposite way and hitting my daughter right between the eyes. Our other two kids took this as a signal to join in and soon there were pieces of food flying left, right and centre. The only one now not joining in was my wife who like an island in a storm picked up her bowl and carried on eating her ice cream, while glaring at us and using her elbow to protect it from being used as ammunition. When a third table joined in we were politely but forcefully asked to leave...

The following morning, my wife was up bright and early having dispatched the two younger children off to their other parents, brought me up a coffee and asked if I would take her shopping in Derby. I mistaking the look she was giving me as 'and in return you will get some nudge nudge, wink wink' agreed. That particular look I have since found out really means 'I have just put mascara on and batting my eyelashes dries it quicker'. As I was begrudgingly corralled out of the house and into the car. It appeared my eldest had received her giro and eager to spend it, had invited herself to join us. There she was sat in the back, waiting like Lady Muck with not even a please or thank you.

Starting the car up, we set off and it soon became clear that my daughter had gas, so much so that every little bump or speed hump would make her go "oops" with a giggle. Driving at 70mph with the windows lowered a little it wasn't that bad. However as we drove through the barrier into the multi-story car park, there was a "Paaarrp!" and a small voice came from the back of the car "I am really sorry for that one...my bad!" It stank to high heaven and had me and her mother racing for the electric windows, but this 'thing' clung on and the higher up the floors we went, the worse it got. With tears streaming down my face, from the heinous gastric expulsion I abandoned the car in the first available space and exited the car with alarming speed. As we headed for the lift, she was stopped by her mother, and told in no uncertain terms, there was no way on earth she was going in that lift with us, and we would meet her at the bottom of the stairs.

We were grateful when she said she would go off to do her own thing and meet us later. We not wanting her to blow all her money in one quick frenzy but also not wanting her to follow us round dropping her guts readily agreed. As just me and my wife headed off to what was then called the Eagle Centre, I tried to relax but with the crowds of idiots that can't walk in a straight line, the sudden stopping with no warning, and others dodging in and out soon had me fuming. As we mounted the steps to the entrance I was ready for the next flappy-eared, sheep-loving, Derbyshite numpty to cross my path. Here he was... a man coming towards us, realising we would be at the glass doors at the same time, looked me in the eye and I knew he wasn't going to slow down. In fact judging by the smile slowly creeping across his face he obviously thought it would be funnier if he hit the door at speed, which would have probably bowled my wife over and I wasn't about to let it happen.

Now I was brought up with manners, I will always open a door for a lady and I will always allow a lady to go first, that said I do expect a thank you, as is the common courtesy, I always try to say please and thank you. This young man however didn't seem to know about manners or if he did, he didn't want to use them. Trying to overt disaster I lengthened my last stride and I jammed my booted foot between the ground and the door just a millisecond before he slammed first his hand then his face and body into the door and like in the cartoons his face was of shocked surprise as he slowly oh so slowly slid down the glass, his nose pawing at the glass as it squealed its way down, finally he fell over to his backside at which point I removed my foot. Opening the door, bowing for my wife to enter, she being the concerned hard as nails Yorkshire lass she is, stepped over him and continued on to the shops without a backwards glance. Me feeling it was too good an opportunity to miss I stopped and leaned over him " you ok son?" he nodded " that looked like it hurt?" he nodded again, smiling like a Cheshire cat I hurried to catch my wife up.

My wife was determined to go in every shop and buy nothing!!! Why? Why would you do that? Is it a female thing or do men do this as well? And when I asked her why, she tells me she is just looking!!! We even went in Contessa and to be honest I thought I would have enjoyed that one more, but all that happened was me going bright red at all these ladies under garments and not knowing where to put my eyes, all the time thinking why do they keep this shop so hot!! I was sweating like a pig at a barbeque. Well that's not shopping then is it? That's just some weird form of torture surely?

We must have gone in over a hundred shops, all of them clothes shops. Not one I wanted to go in like Curry's or Virgin Mega store. And then we went back to the first shop and buy the first thing she had looked at. She also did the "Oh you need some new jeans!" "Do I? When was that decided?" Oh it's not a discussion it's an order!!! I now have some new black jeans with buttons at the front you know like the 501's back in the 80's and every time I need a pee,

I do that silly stand on my tiptoes dance as I fumble to get my buttons and belt undone quickly, instead of just being able to undo my zip. I have come so close to peeing myself because I have forgotten I have these jeans on so many times on it's not funny anymore

After eight hours of idiot dodging I was fuming, she also decided we didn't need to eat and ignored my pleas for a Burger King. In the last shop I couldn't resist any longer, and as the young cashier asked if we needed a bag, I stared meaningfully and nodded towards my wife and answered "No thanks, I have already got one!" I had in fact about fifteen of them and only one was mine. Enough was enough, my feet were aching, my belly was rumbling and I had arms like an orang-utan, "I don't care if you kill me...I want to go home NOW!" I blurted out.

We left the shop in silence, summoned the daughter to the car and drove home in silence. In fact it was only on the Sunday did we start talking again, and that was for her to declare "we were having a clean out". Armed with bin bags she attacked the wardrobes, after three bags, I noticed it only seemed to be my clothes we were clearing...to make room for all her new ones. I only just managed to rescue my favourite Cuban Cars Tee-shirt from being shredded for rags to clean the wardrobe mirrors with.

But hey-ho at least we were now on talking terms again. I am sorry to say at the rate she keeps doing this I will be down to a shopping bag of clothes instead of an eighth of a wardrobe. But what man needs more than a pair of stupid button-fly jeans, a cool tee-shirt and a few underpants and socks anyway? And yet after all this I still worship the ground she walks on; in her brand new, expensive, brown leather, buckled, knee-length boots.

RED KITE TOURING PARK
WHICH WAY THE WIND BLOWS

It was the day before the eagerly awaited event and the time was 6am, the alarm annoying went off, shooting out of bed like a man possessed, I got ready and shot off to work. My work day passed in a flash of me racing around like an idiot and soon I was home. With eager anticipation I could not wait to get going on my four day holiday. I had packed my things in thirty seconds flat. Unfortunately the wife was at work till late, so by seven in the evening I had done all I could and all that was left was to try to get some sleep with the hope of making an early start, but like when I was a kid on Christmas Eve, sleep was nowhere to be found. At 11pm the wife came home and I having had at best thirty minutes sleep was woken with a coffee. Bleary eyed with drool dripping off my chin I slowly came round.

We decided to go get a shop in for the outing so at 1:30am we were to be found sleep-walking round Asda. Putting in anything and everything we fancied and as it's the wife's birthday (and I might get lucky) I sneaked in a bottle of champers and some strawberries, along with lots and lots of treats. The wife being the only sensible one was putting in bread, cooked meats, milk, coffee, pizzas and all other boring things. And even though we were pretty much the only people there I still managed to lose her. With the lack of sleep I had got a tiny bit grumpy, and bravely told her if she ran off again, I would go out to the car and get the dogs lead and make her wear it. I have to be honest I don't know what came over me and I am not sure all the accidents I had on that shopping trip were real ones or just conceived by my wife as punishment. I know anyone can lose their balance and reach out for support, but four times in three minutes is stretching it a bit and each time I ended up knocking stuff off the shelves or using my head as a brake. The trolley hitting my ankles several times started to give me a clue that she did not like my vocal out bursts.

That said Nan's need list has gone down some, we now have a TV-DVD combi, some new knives and forks, two heaters, one an oil filled, the other a blower, as we have no idea which would be the best and having read that some hook ups are low amp we went with both just in case. Oh we also have a mat which I had no idea we needed or when it got on the list, so glad we had a chat about that! Paying for it all we set off for home. We had a quick coffee and then loaded the old girl up. Now we have found the quickest way, though if I am honest not always the best way is for my wife to be in the back of Nan shouting out her demands and for me to run round the house like a headless chicken, grabbing her orders. It always feels like I am in some crazy Wii Fit Game as I puff, pant and wheeze round the house. My wife can fit in Nan and moves around like a ballerina while I, having more mass, tend to crash around like a Sumo wrestler.

Finally Nan is loaded and with items stuffed into every orifice, she is the heaviest she's ever been. Making eye contact with the wife and seeing her give the 'I am ready' nod, apprehensively I head into the house to let forth the explosion that is our dogs, and like two crazed asylum seekers they race with all speed into the back of Nan. As the two of them whip their tails round and bounce about in excitement, and being conscious of the neighbours sleeping at that time, there were soon stifled shouts from my wife. "Harry No!!" "George. On your bed!!" "Harry Sit!...No not on my foot!!!" "George get over there" "Will you both LIE DOWN!!!!" Nan rocks alarmingly from the battle of woman verses dogs, going on inside her, as she tries to get them both settled, I smiling at the image of this fight in my mind, wait outside anxiously for the victor to emerge. Finally my wife, nursing bruised legs and feet, climbed out the door and slammed it shut. "Right, I think we are ready" she wheezed breathlessly.

Getting into the front driver's seat and while I have said this before, I feel like I am in a cockpit of a spitfire as I pull, push and flick switches to get Nan going. Finally Nan coughs into life and as its 4:30 in the morning there is no shouting of FREEDOM!!! But as I have the choke wrong we do start a new craze of bouncing, jumping and skipping down the road, me not wearing a bra raised some concern that I would get a black eye from my energetically moving moobs, while my wife wearing the latest in over-shoulder-bolder holders with added armour plating sat there with regal like composure. The dogs however were heard to shout "more paw less claw" and dancing to the tune of "ring a ring of roses, we all fall down."

With a bit more sticking my tongue out and closing one eye, I got the choke right and our journey started. Now as I have said earlier Nan was the heaviest she has ever been since we have had her, and by golly she was letting me know she was not happy about the extra weight she had put on. We painfully climbed the hill out of our village in first gear and at the summit, I wanted to keep with the tradition of screaming "freedom!" but as we set off down the other side, it ended in a high pitched Alvin and the Chipmunks wail as Nan's brakes did little in the way of stopping us at the lights.

Heading down the A52 my left my foot on the brakes to get the rust off Nan's drums, that's right, Nan is from a time when they used four drum brakes instead of discs. After a time they started to bite better and following our Death wish 2000 we set off into Derby with me asking all the time why it wanted to send us this way, but still following its directions like a lemming. So we headed into the city, with it now being five in the morning it was quiet with Nan wallowing all over the road in self-pity and every bloody light being on red, which meant I had to run the gauntlet of Nan's hide and seek first gear.

Leaving Derby we were soon plodding down the duel carriageways with Nan doing her 'happy speed' of 50mph, the miles on the satnav started to drop. All was going well until the mean trucks came out to play, Nan being the hussy she is was waving her rear end at every passing vehicle bigger than a small van.

After a time my wife showing nerves of steel even went to sleep and there was no warning that we had entered Wales, no sign, nothing!!! However, we must have as through the dim light of early dawn, the views turned picture perfect, with rivers of fog hanging in the valleys, and mountains ranges lurking black and forbidding appearing out of the gloom. Even my wife, snoring with head back and mouth wide open could not detract from the awesome scenes. The roads however, needed my full time attention as they soon became death defying slaloms and wanting to live, Nan's speed dropped to a time consuming 25mph. My expletives along with Nan's ponderous cornering caused the wife to awaken, reaching for the flask she poured us each a coffee and "ooohed" and "aaahhed" as she admired the glorious views. As the road turned into a particularly spectacular valley she grabbed her phone, to take pictures for our Facebook page, setting it to camera. There was a click ...."oh great, a tree" then another click "another tree!" frantically trying to get a decent picture before we went passed, she set the camera to continuous shot and held down the button click...click...click...."Forest!!! F*%K IT!!!!!" So I am sorry to say there will be no pictures of our trip here.

As we entered the small town near our site we found we had hit the Welsh countryside rush hour; three cars, a bike and a bus. Then after a wrong turn into the static caravan park where my wife had to turn her hand to being a banks man to help me with a fifteen point-turn to get back out we finally made it to Red Kite. The site was beautifully laid out in tiers, the hard standing pitches a little too close together for my liking, but that said, it was immaculate. The grass impeccably manicured with ponds bordered by wild flowers, the arrivals bay with hook-up was spotless, and in fact there was not a bit of rubbish anywhere, not even a fag butt. Me and the wife looked at each other, wondering if our decrepit old Nan was too common for a site like this, thinking that they would come out at any moment to chase us off.

At just after 8:30 the campsite office was opened and I went in to pay, the man behind the counter was a rare find, in that he took the money, sorted my empty gas bottle issue and got me onto a pitch of our choice within seconds. Mind you it was still long enough for me to pick up on his Yam-yam accent (Black Country) and there must have been a discount for them as there were quite a few more of them on this site. This Yam-yam shot round the site on an electric folding bike with an energy for life rarely seen, I felt there was nothing I could pose as a problem that he could not sort, he even brought me a coax cable before I knew I needed one!!! Getting Nan on our pitch, we set up, next to us was a post with clean water, rinsing water, hook up and TV out and also a grey waste drain. We set about pegging the dogs out, making up the bed, filling up the water bottles and putting the kettle on for that all important first cup of coffee.

Sitting and relaxing for the first time in many hours, outside in the unseasonably warm sun with our brews, we watched as a couple packed up their van to leave. Then another, and another, growing concerned that so many people were leaving, we were a little conscious that maybe it was us or the dogs or Nan that had caused offence for the site to empty so quickly. Terry the Yam-yam overseeing it all just laughed explaining it was changeover day. The wife decided it was time to make use of the facilities and headed for the toilet block after a rather unreasonable length of time she returned "OMG! The toilets and showers are amazing, they all have under floor heating and they are so warm...and that's not all there is even a dog-washing room!" All this for the reasonable sum of just £24 per night! The views were awesome and soon I was left in peace as the wife took the dogs for a walk. On returning she asked the site manager Terry if it would be ok to let the dogs off their leads for a run in the neighbouring wood. On hearing the answer of "yes" she turned and the three of them abandoned me once again.

A passing couple (Brummies) took pity on me and stopped for a chat, telling me that, they had just been for a walk down to the village, and how it was just twenty minutes or so away. I made a mental note that if it took semi-professional walkers twenty minutes it must be much too far for a semi-professional trucker. It was at this point I got a visitor, a lovely lady with a gentle welsh lilt asked "which one of us was the fifteen stone trucker then?", looking round in panic for my wife who had still not yet come back from her second jaunt after two hours!!! I fought the urge to run away and hide, not because this lady was scary but because I am nothing without my wife holding my backbone straight. Finding myself without back up I entered into light hearted chat and to be honest I was in awe of this lady who had read about our adventures in Nan and gone out of her way to actually come and meet us. Here she was, talking to me, lowly me!!!

Thinking back now I hope I didn't come across as too much of an idiot. My wife came back and within seconds they were chatting, my wife quickly taking to this lovely lady as she had started the conversation with "ah so you are the long suffering wife then?" I get the feeling people really do feel sorry for her. Having met Gorgeous George and Haribo Harry, she had a 'selfie' taken with Nan, before having to rush off back to work. I would like to take this moment to say it was lovely to meet her, and how impressed I was that she could name all the Welsh towns, villages and counties, even that long one that never seems to end without spitting in my face once. While I not wanting to embarrass myself stayed on safe ground, using words like Bala, Shrewsbury and Nottingham. I also would like to wish her all the luck in the future with her dreams of going full time motor homing. As the afternoon wore on we relaxed in the sun which for the middle of October was surprisingly hot. Watching all the newcomers pull up in their cars and caravans, going through all the hassle of moving it into place, setting it up and erecting their awnings.

My wife being a five foot nothing, light weight wuss, was soon three sheets to the wind and on only two very small glasses of wine no less. Now after being awake for over thirty six hours it was decided we would go in and get a few hours kip. Now as you know we sleep in the over cab bed and as I am out of practice, I did have a bit of a struggle climbing up the five feet gap onto the memory foam mattress, my legs going this way and that as I try to get up on my belly, this soon had my wife laughing and telling me that from the rear, I looked very much like a walrus. My wife as ever is watching me from behind and in her mind I am sure she thinks she's being helpful as she states in her dulcet northern tones " There he blows, fine on the forward bow " before climbing like the funky gibbon to join me .

Having slept on some of the four hour journey my wife was soon awake and clambering over me, got down and set off to walk the dogs again! I, rolling into her warm spot, went back to the land of nod. An hour or so later she comes back and because she is awake all must be awake as she and the dogs move round Nan with bird like movements. You know the ones where you pretend to try to creep around but end up rocking the whole van and I was left clinging on to the bed for dear life. In time she tired of this torture and moved to plan B, this plan involved her climbing back into bed this time top to tail and proceeded to rock the bed, pulling the duvet down off my shoulders then kicking it back with her feet. Tossing and turning until she managed to pull it off my feet. She than decided she should have gone to the loo, and climbed back out. By this time the evening had dropped cold, she was freezing, the bed was freezing and I (after our first night camping at Bala, where I had a very bad experience in which I tried to saw myself in half using only some brand new M&S Boxer shorts) now sleeping naked, was also freezing.

As she came out of the toilet, showing her mock surprise at seeing me now awake, she put the kettle on. Me having found myself rudely awakened and very, very cold, was grumpy and not my normal happy-go-lucky self, whether it was from lack of sleep or a painful bloated feeling I know not. As I came round slowly drinking my coffee and smoking a cig, feeling very sorry for myself, I suggested she might like to try our new heaters out. I watched in horror as to my mind it was like one of David Attenborough's Nature films where the female of the species attacks some poor unsuspecting creature, in seconds there was shredded packaging everywhere, the boxes didn't stand a chance.

Slowly Nan started to warm up, and as my wife cleared away the mess we had made throughout the day to make using the heater safer, and having to move things about to set out beds for the dogs, wash up and all those other annoying jobs. Nan starts with the rocking again, with me balancing the coffee in one hand and holding myself steady with the other, in a very small space unable to sit up and ride out the storm of her moving about Well all the wobbling about was making me windy, within minutes I let off the first of many of what I first thought of as harmless and pain relieving botty burps. Well, all I can tell you, is with the fan heater on, these little escapes turned into nose killing odours and each one worse than the last. Soon this had my wife screaming and swearing while opening and closing Nan's back door. Her carrying on like that only started to make me laugh, which in turn caused me to let loose more of these evil odours, the more I laughed the more I let go, I soon had a loud Gatling gun sound going on.

My wife became very insistent that I got out of the bed and went and got rid of what ever had climbed up my bottom and died. With that look in her eye that brokered no argument I did as I was told. While I went to try and sort out my slight problem, my wife had shot back into the safety of the bed. When I eventually came back from the toilet having failed miserably, she seeing and hearing my failure, in turn refused to let me back up into the bed. So there I sat drinking my coffee and every few minutes letting go another bombshell, neither me nor my wife dare light a cig as neither of us wanted to blow the bloody van up, and as the fan heater grabbed hold and heated up these bundles of toxic waste it only got worse. The dogs with a pack like thought moved en masse to hide away in the front cab of Nan.

My wife taking pity on the dogs and her nose became very insistent upon me moving to and standing by, the draft that is Nan's back door, here I was to open and close the door as each pain reliving squeak arrived while at the same time trying to keep the heat in. After a few hours of me thinking I was dying, the wife fell asleep or fell unconscious I know not which and the dogs having fallen silent with only a soft whimpering after each of my chart topping releases, left me to pass the wee hours of the night rocking back and forth and mumbling with a face screwed up in agony "I'm h-a-pp-y (squeak)...I know I am (bellow) I'm sure I am (pop) I'm h-a-pp-y".

WET WILD AND WINDY

The next morning my wife is up and out with some amazingly grateful dogs and I am left all on my own. To be honest I was waiting for the man that runs the site to come knocking on my door and tell me that the other campers had heard me breaking wind after nine o'clock at night and had signed a petition to get me to leave. But no, while I did see him, he just waved from a distance, in a way that left me wondering if he knew of my troubles from last night. As the day wore on, with no sign of my wife or the dogs, I started to get the feeling I had been abandoned, had she finally come to her senses and left me? Had my bottom pushed her too far?

There I was sitting in my old Nan looking out of the window like a forlorn child, awaiting her return, even working on my Facebook posts was not helping. After what seemed like days, hunger got the better of me and I responded to my screaming belly with the hopes of shutting it up. Using my hunter gatherer skills I found my favourite, 'feel sorry for myself' food of mushy peas with mint sauce and vinegar and 'OK' in hindsight it may not have been the best choice of food when camping in a small camper van called Nan. To be fair it has now been banned, along with baked beans, from being consumed while I am on holiday with my wife. After three bowls of this stuff (you so need to try it...only might be best not to while camping) and trying to get back into my wife's good books, I even washed up and put away.

At just after two in the afternoon my wife came back and I, pleased to see her, shot up like a jack in the box to put the kettle on, but in my excitement I had forgotten to clench. My wife on hearing me, just looked at me with daggers, opened a cupboard, grabbed a few packets of crisps, a fruit and nut bar and left again. Oh well coffee for one then. The rest of the afternoon I spent setting up the TV/DVD combi and then testing it by watching a DVD. The pain from the day before still had not gone away and once the film finished I once again set off to the toilet block to see if I could exorcise the demon. My wife was right the toilet block was very clean and warm, even the toilet roll was easy to reach. So inviting was it, that I forgot what I had gone there to do and had a lovely hour sat on the throne just reading my kindle, anyway there was no way I was going to mess up the pristine toilet.

Heading back to Nan with a numb bum and a slight limp from having my foot go to sleep, I was overjoyed to find my wife had returned. However the feeling was not mutual and I was made to sit outside with the dogs as she banged and bashed around opening every window and door to let in as much fresh air as Nan could handle. She was making pizza for the evening meal and even though on several occasions I offered to help, I was told "hell no she wanted to eat food that was not contaminated with my clingy odour and any self-respecting man would have crawled off into the woods and died by now". Just before the pizzas were ready she came out, licked and held up her finger, to check which way the wind was blowing and then I was made to sit, downwind of the whole campsite and more embarrassingly several feet away from the dogs, table and her. So there we sat miles apart from each other in the winter sunshine, watching the world go by and enjoying the views.

To onlookers I would have looked the model of a person relaxing and enjoying himself. On the inside however it was a totally different story, my brain was going into overdrive as it controlled my relaxed expression and the chewing and swallowing of my food, while trying its best to ignore the fire ball of pain that was my belly. Then to top it all off there was the fart-hotline that was my backbone talking my panicking bottom step by step though every relief giving burst of gas..."OK, OK another coming...now ease and squeeze...too loud– shut off...I repeat-shut off!!! Roger that...OK try again...phew...got away with that one...Next one coming...same as before...what do you mean it's jammed open? Clench!! God damn it CLENCH!!" Thinking back now and cringing, that entire whoop-whooping like a world war two destroyer might not have been all in my imagination. As at this point, my wife who is leaning over my shoulder reading this, tells me it was more like having tea with a Yorkshire brass band warming up in the next field.

Oh really? It's OK for you to poke fun at me, but it's not OK for me to say anything when you come home after an eight hour shift at M&S and for the next two hours walk round the house like a Tyrannosaurs Rex trying to fool me into thinking every roar is coming out of your mouth!! Or when you sit on the settee in the conservatory smoking a cigarette with 6ft flames shooting out, do you really think I fall for the "it's Puff the magic fire breathing dragon!!!" That said, going back to the site, where I am sat outside eating my pizza I did think that I had discovered some Welsh cricket like insect that every minute or so would let out a "Tut" like noise, but when my wife and dogs got up to go into Nan they seemed to have scared it away. Getting up to follow them in, I made it all the way to Nan's back door before my eyes met my wife's eyes and she let me know without a word being spoken that, in no uncertain terms I was to even set one foot in Nan. As the door closed in my face I sighed, turned round and walked back to my chair, helped along by my gas powered buttocks, making the sound of a whoopee cushion as I sat back down in disgrace.

I watched my wife close every window, door and sky light then all the curtains. Was she kicking me out? Should I go sleep in the toilets? The sun had now set and the temperature had dropped to what in my mind were arctic conditions, with teeth chattering I looked into the dark sky wondering 'Why me lord?' It was then that I noticed all the stars, so many of them, billions of them, such a beautiful and unforgettable memory. It always fills me with an odd sadness, knowing I will never get to go to any of them and how wonderful it is that in my life time we might make it to Mars. It really hits it home, just how insignificant we really are. What a destructive and inward looking species we are becoming, and how the cost of the dream is more important than the glory of getting it to come true. Added to that all the new technology that is killing the art of conversation, all leaves me feeling so old and out of touch with society.

I am brought back to earth with a thump to the ribs and a cup of coffee thrust into my hands, quickly grabbing the hot drink I watch my wife looking up at the sky, taking the opportunity I cosy up behind her, knowing very well she too is wondering when will we be able to move to Scotland and stay up late watching stars without worrying about the rat race that is our life at the moment. I loved holding her in my arms, for me that was the best twenty minutes of the whole trip. That was until she went back into her Yorkshire, hard-as-nails, ice-queen mode. "Come on, I ain't standing out here freezing when there's a TV ta watch" and with that she shot off back into Nan, with one more glance at the stars I turned to follow her. Getting back into Nan it was all warm and cosy, the dogs were asleep on their beds, and the heater was working a treat.

My wife had commandeered my laptop and had Emmerdale on catch up. She had also opened her champagne and strawberries and it all looked romantic with the few candles she had lit. Not over sure if I was forgiven I stripped down to my birthday suit and helped by my gas powered bottom made my best time into the bed. Tonight's cutting remark from my wife was "It's life Jim...but not as we know it". Sticking my tongue out at the back of her head, I settled down on my 5ft high perch, the rest of the evening passed by in a haze of pain, gas and continuous back to back Emmerdale. I also found that, the Welsh cricket thing that 'Tuts' had somehow got into the van and made a mental note to try and find it in the morning.

I must have drifted off as the next thing I knew I was woken by my bed rocking alarmingly and I came round to find my wife powering down the lap-top and going to the toilet. As she stripped down to her underwear, I wondered when all her pretty sexy underwear had been replaced by armour plated bras and belly warmer knickers. Oh yes probably when she got an M&S discount card! Rocking back and forth on her tip toes like an athlete does before the high jump, she says "mind out".

I don't even get chance to move before her face is an inch from mine and a steel hardened knee cap is in my man dangles. As our heads bash together, the air races out of my lungs and my knees go up to my chest. Rubbing her head she rolls off and onto her side of the bed, once again catching me in the now very tender sad sack and road kill that was my manhood. All thoughts of being amorous are well and truly gone as I rocked side to side cupping my injured parts while mewing in pain.

As with all aspects of my life, I do seem to have more than my fair share of bad luck in that department, we used to have a great sex life...once. But after a string of bad experiences, like the time my wife brought a sexy Mrs Santa outfit as a surprise that she had for me in the bedroom one night. Me like the other well-known jolly fat fellow with a beard and full sack that only comes once a year was very eager but as she bent over encouraging me things went wrong. As I felt the velvet like texture of the outfit I yelped, my hands constricted into claws, my teeth set on edge and my body started shuddering all over. My wife looking round to see what all the fuss was about, seeing my reaction to touching the velvet started to laugh so much so that she ended up on the floor crying. Swearing on all that was holy that she had forgotten about my 'Sensory Processing Disorder' and the odd little foible of me being completely unable to touch it.

The other thing that comes to mind is when she decided to use a ping-pong bat as a sex paddle and somehow managed to persuade me into bending over naked. So there I was stooped over my hands holding my knees and at first it was going well her being all gentle, but within seconds the hilarity of it over took her and each smack was getting harder and harder as she howled with laughter. Until she hit me with so much force I fell over, as my hands touched the floor a pain unlike any I have ever felt before exploded from my man dangles then shot like a bullet straight into my head and as I blacked out, I swear I heard her shout "fore!!!" The latest time was not long after we got Nan and we decided to christen it, so to speak. After a few drinks we decided tonight was the night (we...I really mean she!) As I set off to un-lock Nan, she grabbed the book of sex positions someone had given us as a joke a few years ago.

Within minutes we were on the 5 foot bed flicking through the pages, many of the positions needed more space than we had, so we plumped for the 69. For those that don't know it's where you face each other, only top to tail, me mouthing the alphabet and her batting away at a wasp. All was going well until I got to the letter S, then she let one off. Me being a gentleman was trying my hardest to carry on even though my eyes were watering but ended up having to start at A again. This time I got to G before she let off again. That was it! I spun round until we were face to face and told her there was no way I was going to take another 67 of them!!! Oh how we laughed, me because I thought I was being funny, her because she was going to make me pay for this for a very, very long time. Well the 'tutting' cricket thing had moved some where very near the bed, but it now seems to have stopped when the wife began snoring. As my pain eased to where my eyes stop watering, I finally drifted off to sleep.

OCTOPUSSY

I wake very early as I am in so much pain, getting down off the bed and dressing, I put the kettle on. After nipping to the little boy's room I make the coffee, today is the wife's birthday, so as a treat I thought I would make her a full English breakfast. Sitting at the table watching as the mist slowly withdraws from the camp site, I wait for the wife to come back from the dead. Within minutes of smelling the coffee she starts to come round. "Hope you made me one... It is my birthday you know" she growled at me.
"Yes Honey Bun, Happy Birthday my love!"
"I don't do birthdays" she hisses back at me, then the lump that is our duvet starts to move and as I am sitting at the table looking up, what happened next will forever be burned into my mind.

At first the duvet released her petite feet then her shapely calves, then her sexy thighs, while all this is going on I am drooling like a peeping tom, with eyes on stalks and swallowing hard. But as her bum appears all hell breaks loose, what was a very attractive bottom half of a human female in my mind suddenly changed into a two armed octopus waving its tentacles about franticly and I promise you I tried to be a gentleman and I tried not to look at its mouth, but I could not help it. Unable to shut my eyes or stop them moving on their own accord, my eyes unwillingly focused on this things mouth, all the time I am mumbling "Oh God, oh God noooo, oh God.....my eyes!!!" This thing had eaten a lot of spiders!! There were spiders' legs hanging out all around its mouth and then it spoke in a very angry Yorkshire accent "help me then!!"... I could not!!

I could not move I was stuck to the seat in fright, nor could I say a word, in fact, I was frozen in terror, silent screaming terror, the only part of me moving was my bottom doing an amazingly good imitation of a bugler playing the "retreat". At last this nightmare got one of its 'arms' to touch the other seat and it morphed back into my beautiful wife who misinterpreted my smile of relief from not being killed by the monster for one of me being pleased to see her, started to do a sexy little dance and bursts into Rod Stewart's song. My mind answers her:

If you want my body and you think I'm sexy

(Nope not from that angle)

Come on, sugar, let me know

If you really need me, just reach out and touch me

(Not going to happen now I have that image burned into my mind)

Come on, honey, tell me so, tell me so, baby

(No way Spider legs)

With that she slaps me on the forehead and disappears into the loo, she soon comes racing out to get dressed as there is still a chill in the air and the heater doesn't warm that area. We sit drinking our coffee watching the campsite slowly come to life. The wife drains her coffee and gets ready to take the dogs out and for the next few minutes it's pandemonium as coat sleeves, arms, collars and leads fly and the dogs get over excited at the chance to get out and away from me and my un-welcome smells.

Harry is prancing about, hitting me very hard with his lethal whip-like tail as much as he can. Not to be outdone George is using his paws to stomp on my sock covered feet, huffing and puffing and for good measure snorts drool at my face. As the door is flung open and all three charge out into the light, I uncurl from my cowering position with relief.

Getting the kettle on and making another coffee to drown my sorrows with, I am now getting the feeling that even the dogs wished I would go and find a quiet place to die in. I tidy up the van and get ready to make the breakfast, but I can't start the surprise as my wife has deemed it unimportant to inform me of her return time, maybe she thinks I have crystal balls the way she always leaves me guessing at her intentions or that I am a mind reader!!! I do everything I can to be ready the moment she comes back. Three hours later the door crashes open, all the heat is let out as they bound back in to be fed, after which she announces she is going to take George and try out the dog wash.

Now Harry is a Mummy's boy, he doesn't like to share her with George and hates it even more when she takes George out without him (even if it's to go to the vets) so for the next thirty minutes he paces back and forth trying to peek out of the windows to see where they are, trampling me and whipping me, while whimpering and whining which turns into full blown cries as he sees them returning. Nan's door is flung open and a very clean, fluffy but still slightly damp George bursts in. My wife swaps dogs and Harry is pleased to be allowed to go with her this time. George obviously enjoyed the experience and is so very giddy, he invites himself to the space next to me, then on me, wriggling and pushing his way on to my lap then rolling over for his belly rub. He has absolutely no understanding of 'personal space' or the word 'no' either. For the next thirty minutes I cannot move, as I am crushed under an eight stone, soggy lump, but at least he smells pleasant.

The next time Nan's back door flies open, in comes a harassed wife and a much traumatised soaking wet Harry. Harry is the youngest and for some reason he is afraid of everything and I mean everything…my wife had eventually managed to bath him but the hair drier had apparently been far too much for him, she had to towel dry him the best she could.

As she is also now wet and covered in dog hair my wife announced she too would be going for a shower, so after grabbing her toiletry bag and towel she waltzed off. The dogs evidently distressed at her leaving them with the windy human, charge back and forth looking for her. Now with two very big Bull Mastiffs in our very small Nan there is not a lot of room for them to move around, I am whipped, sat on, trod on, crushed and dripped on for another forty five minutes.

When the door opens again my wife enters looking like a model, makeup done, hair all shiny and straight while I, having been pinned up against the window by two cold and wet dogs, looked like a tramp who's done a few rounds with Mike Tyson in some freaky pool wrestling competition. 'Tutting'…it now finally dawns on me that the Welsh cricket thing was her all along; she takes the dogs and pegs them outside.

Feeling it is now safe to stand again, I hobble around the kitchen area making a start on the breakfast or as it now is…dinner (I think posh people call this brunch); sausages, bacon, eggs, fried and tinned tomatoes, mushrooms, baked beans, fried bread, toast and buttered bread. After eight years of being with my wife I have tried to woo her with posh hotels, restaurants and expensive food and now know, much to my dismay, that to get on my wife's good side, she is happiest with the 'greasy spoon' style of cooking.

After the juggling that only those who have attempted to cook a full English in a motorhome will understand, combined with the fact that I am a man and multitasking is not my strongest point, eventually it's ready. I start to plate up, the table is already set with knives and forks, red and brown sauce, coffee and orange juice, oh and a lit candle. With the ball of fire that is still in my belly I only give myself a small portion and heap the rest on my wife's plate knowing full well that if she can't finish it, the dogs will.

I set the two plates down and turn back to butter the bread and toast, before returning to my seat. As I picked up my knife and fork I noticed that I must have forgotten to put baked beans and eggs on my plate, looking over to the now stacked pots and pans the mystery deepened as they were all empty!!! I checked the floor to see if my food had dropped off my plate as I had carried it over... nope! I even looked out of the window to check the dogs had not got loose and sneaked in and stolen it...no, they were still tied up outside. Finally I looked over to my wife's plate to see if I was going doo-lally and had not cooked them at all. Oddly her plate had fried eggs and beans...so where had mine gone???

Grabbing a triangle of toast I stood up and looked over the pots and pans again. It was just as I thought they were all empty of food, sitting back down chewing on said toast I looked at my wife. She was busy wolfing down my cuisine and looking like butter would not melt in her mouth. "I think I am going mad, I could have sworn I put eggs and beans on my plate."
"Aye happen" she replied still eating.

The more I thought about it the more I was positive I had put them on my plate, leaning over and pushing my food around I noticed some baked bean juice, I knew I had!!! So where had it gone?? With my powers of deduction I could only come to one conclusion... and she was avoiding eye-contact.
"Love...do you know where me food went?" Her fork paused on its way to her mouth and hovered there for a second. She fixed me straight in the eye with one eyebrow slightly raised in a warning sign. "Seriously? After the last few days, you really think I am going to let

you eat beans, or eggs? I took them!" It obviously wasn't up for debate; I wasn't having a say in the matter but she did have a fair point if I was honest. I 'took heed' and continued with my food in a mard.

As soon as the meal was finished, my wife perturbed by my strained silence, rolled her eyes then gathered the washing up bowl full of pots and pans and marched off to wash them up. Not to be out-done I gathered up my kindle and also set off to the toilet block to continue my sulk in peace....but also in an effort to rid me of the pain that was ruining my life.

As I enter the toilet block I make my way over to the stalls, two out of the three are in use and because I am very 'public toilet shy' so to speak, I have to resist the urge to turn and run. Forcing myself to enter the last stall I made myself comfy and within moments I must have forgotten I was not alone or maybe it was the relief that something down there was happening but I burst into that Freddie Mercury song...
Don't stop me now,
Don't stop me
Don't stop me
Hey, Hey, Hey
It's burning through my bum at
Two hundred degrees
That's why they call me Mister Shoot-on-site
It's travelling at the speed of light
I wanna make a supersonic boom near you
Don't stop me now; I'm having such a good time,
I'm having a pooooo!
Ooh, ooh, ooh....I like it!!!
Having such a good time...good time.

Still to this day I have no idea what came over me. But it suddenly all came flooding back to me as the guy in the next stall burst out laughing, which in turn set the other guy off. All the while I was going bright red and cursing my stupidity and wondering why I had not turned and run when I had the chance. I was wondering how I was going to get out of the toilets without revealing my identity, when lady luck took pity on me. A deep trombone like noise that somehow echoed round the bowl came from the man in the next cubicle, and set me off giggling, then what in my mind's eye I can only describe as the sound of a baby whale being dropped and a gallon of water hitting the floor in the third stall.

Imagine the scene three grown men howling in laughter like school children, I for one had tears streaming down my face. None of us even noticed the next man enter the building until we heard "Are you guys going to be long?" As I desperately tried to compose myself enough to I reply, my voice wavered "yea, I am about done!" A voice from another stall added
"Are you sure?"
And I lost it again.... "Nope!!"

This set us all off once more, for a full five minutes the block was filled with roars of laughter. Each of us waiting for someone else, to be brave enough to be the first to leave. Regaining my breath and composure and with as much dignity as I could muster, I shot out of the stall like a race horse, galloping as quickly as I could back over the campsite to the safety of Nan.

Puffing and wheezing, I collapsed into the seat across from my wife and as I tried to splutter out the reason for my sudden dishevelled appearance, in between snorts of laughter and soggy tears I could make out the look of despair on her face. "We really can't take you anywhere, can we?" She grabbed up the dog leads, and announced she would take them out one last time before feeding them in the hope they would settle for the evening.

Having time alone to calm down, I realised how much better I was feeling. The pain and wind appeared to have gone; I started to relax, opened a beer to celebrate and took out my laptop to write my next chapter.

As the evening drew in, the weather changed from being unseasonably warm to fecking freezing. A real life Ice-Queen returned from a very blustery walk, her teeth chattering and icicles hanging off her nose. The heaters were soon on full blast and as Nan warmed up, we settled down to pick at what was left in the cupboards for supper along with our coffee refills. The dogs took to their beds, as the wind whistled outside.

There was no Emmerdale entertainment, as the wife tried to make my chapter readable to the human race (that's her reason for checking it and she is sticking to it). After a couple of hours sitting with her feet on a hot water bottle, wrapped in a blanket, pouring over my laptop she declares it safe to post and I set about getting it onto my Facebook page. The dogs are reluctant to go out again, so she resorts to blackmail by stuffing treats in her coat pockets, the van starts rocking as they hurry to get their share, and they eventually leave taking all the heat out with them.

Left on my own, with very little warmth left, I decided now would be a good time to take to the bed, as I stripped down to by birthday suit I smiled to myself at knowing my wife wouldn't see me struggle into the bed tonight. Oh how wrong could I be, the shot of freezing air around my naked buttocks, half way through the climb up to the cab bed, soon let me know how wrong. As the gang pushed their way back into Nan I heard the familiar northern dulcet tones, as I hurried to get under the duvet. "Full moon......half-moon...total eclipse" As I arranged myself to get my head out of the covers, and my body under them, I watched as she sorted the dogs and removed her coat, all the time she was shivering and sniffing back a running nose. "You're SNOT funny" I retorted.

The dogs seemed to be asleep in seconds, as my wife made the last coffee of the day and then nipped to the loo, she came out wearing just my tee shirt and judging by her chest area it was very, very cold, smirking (OK and drooling) I said "you wanna be careful with those, or you will have someone's eye out with them". With ape-like grace she eventually climbs up and over me, I am pretty sure it was my eyes she was trying to poke out.

We had just settled down to drink the coffee, while reading the comments from the Facebook page on my latest post, when my wife starts to complain about her neck and shoulders aching. Taking the hint I get out of the bed and jump down onto Nan's now ice cold lino floor, opened one of the drawers, grabbed the deep heat and raced back into the bed to find my wife laying on her front topless. As I lather her neck, shoulders and back in deep heat part of me wonders why it's never the front that needs cream rubbing in!!!

We settled down to finish our coffee and continue reading the comments and until that night I had never noticed how much I unconsciously adjust my gentleman parts. What started off as a warm glow in my nether region, quickly developed into searing pain that I can only describe as my man dangles being attacked by a blow torch! The deep heat cream that had been left on my hands had rubbed off onto my oldest friend.

Seconds later I was to be found naked squatting on top of the Thetford, dribbling cold water from the kettle over my molten baubles. My wife tucked up warm in bed and clueless to my predicament asked what was I doing, me unable to form a full sentence screamed "HOT BOL......LOCK!!!" there was only the slightest pause as my wife put two and two together and set off howling with laughter. As I leave the toilet to get kitchen roll to dry myself off my wife watching me says "goodness gracious great balls of fire!!!" and falls back down laughing hysterically, not the sympathy I was looking for as I made my way back into bed wondering if my balls were glowing in the dark. Getting under the duvet and making sure there was a draft to my tender parts, my wife snuggled up to my back and nuzzled up to my ear and for a second I thought she was being sympathetic to me until she started to sing in her lullaby whisper "Chestnuts roasting on an open fire" giggling again as she rolled away from me.

It was safe to say I didn't feel the cold that night!

THE CHIPS ARE DOWN

All too soon the morning has come and it's time to depart this beautiful site. The wife is slow to rise and I make the first coffee of the day, all the time never looking in my wife's direction so as to avoid yesterday's nightmare of the spider's legs. That said I have dropped a lot of hints about gardens, bush trimming and mowing.

We sit at the table drinking our coffee, neither of us in a good mood as we have to pack up to go back and re-join the rat race that is life. My style of bad mood is to go quiet and surly, my wife's bad moods are quite the opposite, in that she becomes a hurricane of energy, cutting remarks and shoots out orders like a machine gun. To avoid bloodshed I suggest she takes the dogs for a last walk while I begin to pack up the van. I start with the bed by loading all breakables like my precious laptop, the TV and the heaters and putting pillows round them so they won't break if I brake too hard. I know in Nan this is hard to do, but as I am a trucker it's a habit I can't break. I then move onto loading all the cupboards up with the pots, pans, cups and plates in fact I only leave the kettle; coffee, sugar and two cups out just in case grumpy might need another caffeine hit before leaving.

I then set about pinning the curtains back ready to travel but leave the ones in the driving cab for the wife as she is a black belt in origami and has a set way SHE likes to do them. I sort out the cushions, bases and the table so the dogs have more space and the floor is clear for the wife to sweep. I move outside to check tyres, pack up the chairs, big table and wind break and put them all in their travelling places. Lastly I open Nan's bonnet to check her levels and see if I can spot why, as we neared our destination three days ago she had started to lose power.

Upon hearing the jingle of the dog's chains I look round to see my wife coming back. Now I love this woman dearly, yes I maybe bigger, stronger and uglier than her but she has the one ring to rule them all. She scares me when she is in this mood, I am not going to lie to you, I take one look at her face and run, only stopping long enough to grab my Kindle. Then with a bum like a rabbit's nose I depart for the toilet block to hide, as I turn to look back at poor Nan, I see she is already rocking as my wife attacks her chores like an angry Tasmanian devil. Even our two fearless Bull Mastiffs, know not to get under her feet while she is in this mood, and they are cowering quietly outside.

Actually hiding in the toilet did appear to be quite a good idea; it seems she really does have the ability to loosen my bowels and scare the number two's out of me.

There is only so long you can hide on the toilet, eventually I had to be brave and come out, but not before peeping out of the window first. When I saw her marching towards the toilet block, I thought she was coming to flush me out, until I realised she had the Thetford cassette, and was obviously on her way to empty it. I decided to give her another few minutes just in case she asked me to 'help.' After the episode in Whitchurch I try to give that particular job an extra wide berth.

Feeling slightly guilty at my hide and seek tactics, I follow as she marches back down to Nan, lengthening my stride to catch her up, now here is where I am in greatest danger of her northern blunt tongue lashing and I have to tread very lightly. Risking it all, I use the 'safe' word "coffee?" If she says yes I know we are down to amber alert which means I am not in too much danger and at best there might be some mild pecking.

My luck was in, she agreed, her horns were slowly receding, and the angry expression was fading, she must be happy with the progress she had made already. With all respect she had done well, even draining the grey waste, everything was spick and span. She had even had time to re-do all my earlier packing. I drive a truck and have to make loads safe for transport on a daily basis but rather than get annoyed at her for belittling my efforts of packing Nan up, I let it slide as I have no wish to relight the fuse on her temper.

As I come back out with the coffee, she is nowhere to be seen, I have to check the dogs are still there to know she is somewhere close. I find her with her head buried in Nan's engine compartment, and have to hold back a chuckle...like she has any idea what she looking at!!! As I offer her the cup, she asks "have you sorted it then?" That put me on the back foot, and as I struggled to find the correct answer I stutter "erm, well yes, and erm the liquids seem OK, the oil is about right, I just need to ... I was just going to get my screwdriver ...." I was interrupted by her remarking how dirty all the windows were, and how there was no wonder she couldn't see through her side...or in fact how I managed to see to drive. With a swish of her hair she stormed off for a cloth and washing up liquid, my tool box also suddenly appeared beside me.

She must have decided to start with the insides, as soon Nan began swaying as her glassware was lathered up then wiped down rather enthusiastically. I was then joined back outside as she tackled the door windows and windscreen, while I studied the problem with Nan's lack of get up and go, by my powers of deduction I figured....it had to be the engine! The carburettor looked fine, the fuel filter wasn't blocked. I knew the fault couldn't be electrical as Nan is quite primitive in that department.

As my wife kept glancing expectantly at me as I stood with screwdriver in hand, I thought it best to unscrew something...it was here I discovered that upon opening the air filter compartment, it was completely empty there was definitely no air filter in there. Just how, when or where Nan had lost that I have no idea. I also found black debris indicating Nan's pulleys had been chewing into the cam belt cover, this being sucked into the carburettor would have caused the jets to block. Knowing a few tricks of the trade, I grabbed my trusty can of brake cleaner and set about blasting it clean. Happy I had sorted the problem, admiring my handy work, and giving it a final glance over before I shut down the bonnet...I noticed a small insignificant looking tube hanging down. No big deal I just had to find where it had detached from, but try as I might I could not find anything to reattach it to!!!

Seeing me starting to lose my temper at this stupid piece of pipe, my wife asked "what's up with it?" I replied that "this pipe here, look! Needs to go somewhere, and I can't see where". Being a man the last thing I thought about was reading an instruction manual as this should have been such an easy fix. My wife had scurried off and returned with the Haynes manual and was flicking through like she knew what she was looking for. Rolling my eyes, I took the book off her and turned to the pages showing the carburettor, it looked like it attached to a small outlet nub near the base. However no matter how hard I pushed or squeezed, it was not going on.

Realising that time was getting on and we were expected to be leaving the pitch by now, I was getting really frustrated. This turned to pure anger as I peered at the nub more closely. "The dirty, lowdown, flappy-eared, money-grabbing, grease monkeys, have just snapped the damn thing off. Look it is still stuck inside...there's no way that's going back on there now". Apparently my wife would like me to add here, that I resembled a balding bantam cockerel, strutting about and squawking out high pitched obscenities, "F...F....F this, that and the other" while claiming "well that's it then! It can't be fixed", "the end of the world is nigh", "God knows how I'm supposed to drive home now".

My wife, getting bored of me and my meltdown, leant in to have a closer look at the offending pipe, suggesting that we might try to remove the broken piece. Her being a lot smaller in stature than me was obviously able to get in nearer, so near in fact that she was able to point out that there seemed to be another 'sticky-out-bit' a little further up and asked what if she attached it there then? Well she just had to be right didn't she? She didn't have to gloat about it though! Or close up my toolbox with such a smug expression! I have no idea how she got that big-head of hers into the cab of Nan, but very soon we were ready for the off.

Nan jumped to attention straight off the key, and was purring like a kitten, as I pulled up by the site office to let Terry the Yam-yam know we were going. Turning her off, I jumped out to go and hand the aerial cable back in. Having said our goodbyes I hopped back in and began going through the spitfire start up sequence.... nothing. I tried again, Nan refused to fire into life. And again....nope! In fear of flooding the engine, I gave her a few minutes, and then tried again...not a sausage! I looked at my wife, she looked back at me. Both wondering how she had just died, after managing to drive so well all the way up the hill.

My over active imagination went off on one again, the embarrassment of having to be rescued by the AA off this posh site. The humiliation of Nan's return journey being on the back of a recovery truck. How the wobble-box owning neighbours who had scoffed at our decrepit old van, would laugh, seeing her dumped unceremoniously on our drive.

My wife reached to get her AA card and phone from her purse. I pleaded with Nan in desperation "Come on baby, light my fire", "let's go home", "please ... just for me". And then it dawned on me, I had missed one teeny tiny little switch, and like all women it had been enough to not turn her on. Half way through my wife dialling the AA rescue number Nan roared into life, and me not wanting to admit that it had been my fault all along, feigned fake surprise, and marvelled how lucky we were. My wife like a dog with a bone, wouldn't let it go, and even when I tried to distract her with all the lovely views, insisted I tell her what I thought the problem might have been. "Oh all right it was me... I made a mistake...yes, another one...I forgot a switch! Happy now?"

Down through the village, up the hill at the other side, and out into the wonderful Welsh countryside, we sped. And for the first couple of hours I had to listen to my wife remarking how brilliantly Nan seemed to be driving, and whether I thought it was the pipe she had fitted that had made the improvements...over and over again!

Reluctantly I did have to agree, Nan seemed to have better braking, more power and there was no more of that bucking and jerking she had previously done every time we set off from a stand still. In fact Nan had so much power that for the first time ever since owning her, we actually over took several trucks and a wobble-box...twice, just because we could! Nan's 'happy speed' increased from 50mph to 55mph and at one point she even crept over 60mph and set a new personal best record of 62mph. We also had a little celebration as Nan turned 80...well reached 80,000 miles on her clock. The journey home was pretty much hassle free and really quite enjoyable.

Apart from the time I stopped to fill up Nan's thimble size tank and the wife spotting a fish and chip shop, decided that she was hungry and we would have some for dinner. She leaped out while I was doing the petrol...so I waited there on the pump, as I had finished and paid. Not daring to pull away from the pump as there was nowhere else I could fit Nan...I waited. Trying to ignore the glares of other drivers as I blocked up the whole forecourt waiting! I don't even like fish and chips!

Twenty whole minutes it took them to fry chips, my wife never even glanced in my direction, so I could gesture to her to hurry up. For the first time in my life I was truly grateful I had two large Bull Mastiff faces pressed up and drooling down my windows, they seemed to be deterring the locals from haranguing me. Finally my wife skips out of the shop oblivious to my peril, jumps in and states "let's hope she starts this time eh, are we eating these here? Or finding a park or something?"
"Yes or something" I replied, starting the engine in record time and getting Nan to do a wheel spin which was another first, as we shot out of the petrol station like a rocket.

My wife completely unaware of how close we came to being lynched was floundering bewilderedly trying to fasten her seat belt while trying not to lose her prize fish and chips to the dogs. I put a good fifteen miles between us and that petrol station before I dared to pull over into a lay-by. I am sorry to say that even with copious amount of vinegar and tomato sauce from Nan's cupboards the fish and chips had not been worth all the anxiety. And even more disappointing was my wife's refusal to attempt to drive Nan home, so I could buy the fabulous Jaguar XKR soft top which is one of my dream cars that was unbelievably for sale in the same lay-by.

Getting Nan back on the drive I have to say that after all the excitement of our four day break I really could use a holiday to recover.

A MANUAL WOULD BE NICE

This chapter is about another of my failed attempts to wow/woo my wife. Just because I put a ring on it doesn't mean my job is done, nowhere near. That said it would make life a lot easier if it was. My wife of eight years, soon to be nine, takes great pride in her Northern upbringing and even more pride in being from Yorkshire. She has an A level in sarcasm, a few O levels in cutting remarks and hard put downs, in fact she takes great pride in being a northern hard as nails ice queen and works so hard to maintain it. I, on the other hand, was born in Yorkshire but was raised in Nottingham so have lost a lot of my northernness and I am best described as insecure, cheeky and standoffish. I have a defence wall a mile high and she is the only one to have ever walked though it like it didn't exist, in doing so she stole my heart.

To say I worship the ground she walks on would be an understatement, we do work well together and even on the days we fall out and can't even look at each other the love is clear for all to see. I am never ashamed to tell all that will listen that I love her and she's with me. However, my wife on the other hand, finds displays of emotion beyond her, being soppy is a sign of weakness and the words "I love you" should only be said to her dogs, chocolate and new Vacuum cleaners (wife snorts in northern derision and says that at least they are useful). We approach things differently too. I am very softly, softly catchee monkey where she is the bluntness of the Yorkshire hammer and let's kill said monkey!!

We do have friction points like all couples. I like to plan and think about how I will get it done right first time, my wife is more the roll your sleeves up, jump in then getting mad at it and scare everyone into getting it done. I have to be honest her way works more times than it fails; she is the realist I am the dreamer.

I am open and happy to chat, she is quiet and hides her thoughts. I am touchy feely and without her saying a word I know she would say you are more like something I trod in and can't get off my shoe. She is "you can only touchy feely me feet" or "rub my shoulders" and no more!!! A true Queen and I am her happy servant. That said there are times when I go the extra mile to make her feel appreciated and end up feeling hard done by. Here is just one of many stories which comes to mind.

The first one which I will share with you now was on her fortieth a few weeks before I had asked our eldest to sort a surprise party out in Huddersfield where my wife had moved from to come live with me. The daughter agreed with much gusto and put it out on Facebook, little did we know at the time but that was as far as it got. The 'secret' post she had put up, hidden so my wife wouldn't see it, was so secret that no-one else saw it either. The day arrived and I took the wife clothes shopping ready for the big night, she had already agreed to take the middle child to see her Dad so she was going up anyway. It was as she was getting ready that our eldest came clean and told us that no party was happening. She literally couldn't organise a pee up in a brewery!

It was no good the wife had to drive up there and drop off the other child, she said she was OK with it and would pop into her mums for a cup of tea and a chat. The eldest, thinking this was better than watching TV all night, showed more brass than a brass monkey in that she invited herself along. I don't know how my then new wife felt about all of this as she is good at hiding her true feelings. But I was fuming and as they loaded themselves into the car I vowed to make it right.

Swinging into action like the rusty knight I am, I shot into my car, raced round to Tesco's and went on the hunt for all the things I needed to give her a night to remember. However, abandoning the car, grabbing a trolley and then racing into the supermarket only to find when I got to there, I had no idea where the things I wanted were or if they even sold them!!! I grabbed the nearest member of staff, told her what I wanted to do and begged her to help, within seconds I had three young girls racing round the supermarket grabbing the things I needed off the list, soon my trolley was full and I thanked them for their help. I was told by them that they wished their men were so romantic. With this endorsement ringing in my ears what could go wrong? Racing to the check out, I paid for the goods then shot to the car, loaded it all in and raced home.

Tonight's treat for her was going to be in our newly decorated front room, lighting our brand new fire and closing the curtains I set about preparing for her return. I spent over an hour laying out a fleece blanket down in front of the fire, and placing lots of candles round the room and not just any candles these were them scented ones!!! I undid the wrapping of the Thornton's chocolates and laid them out along with a Vanilla all over body cream. Shooting to the kitchen I grabbed all the vases we owned, all three of them and filled them each with twelve roses one with white, one pink and the last red then set them out round the front room. Heading back to the kitchen to put the strawberries in a fancy bowl and into the fridge along with the champagne then washing the new champagne glasses I had just brought. By now I was sweating like a pig at a barbeque, sending a text to see where my wife was and getting one back telling me she was on her way. I raced for the shower. Teeth cleaned, body washed and dried I had shaved, combed my hair and I shot into the bedroom to get ready.

In one of the drawers was a novelty pair of men's sexy underpants, now I use the word underpants very loosely as these are better described as a garrotte and pouch, a very small pouch, I spent five minutes just figuring out how I was to get into these things, even looked on the internet to see a picture of how they were to be worn. Finally after much swearing and grunting I managed to get these things round my waist, looking in the mirror I have to say I could not see what women would find attractive about them, they did very little to hide my modesty and most of my bits were oozing out the sides along with a lot of spiders legs. This wasn't what the look I wanted!!! Hobbling back into the bathroom and grabbing my razor I set about hacking the spider's legs off. I only wanted to trim it a little but within minutes I have shaved myself bald and now in my mind's eye down there looked like a freshly plucked chicken.

Grabbing the aftershave I pour some into my hand and slapped it onto my face and I don't know what possessed me to then put, only a small amount mind you, onto my man dangles. The pain that followed was immense and had me doing my best Indian war dance yet, even managing to do the yowls at the right time. With one hand I was trying to waft cold air down onto the inferno that was my manhood the other hand trying to stop the cheese cutting string sawing up my bottom.

Unfortunately the hand I used to do this was still covered in aftershave and while I don't want to go into too much detail, that Johnny Cash song sums it up well.... "It burns, burns, burns...my rings on fire!!" It took twenty minutes for the burning to stop and a further five for me to stop crying. Making my way back into the bedroom I give myself the once over in the mirror, starting at the top; hair....great. Face....nice close shave. Teeth...clean. Swollen and red eyes...starting to clear. Chest...moobs look sexy... Now I would like to say six pack but as I drive a truck for a living I have long since lost that and hover between the family pack and the bulk buy. Small black triangle of black nylon cutting into my flesh...check!! Thin legs and knobbly knees…check!! All finished off with pasty white Day-Glo skin, this was as good as I would get without mass surgery and a spray tan.

Checking the time I saw I had fifteen minutes or so before she got back and put on my white towelling dressing gown I had got from Nescafe after saving all them beans up. Slowly I made my way down the stairs trying not to anger the garrotte into adventuring further up into the unknown. Like a duck I waddled into the front room and lit the candles then into the kitchen to get the strawberries out and put them next to the chocolates in the front room, it all looked warm and romantic.

I did pat myself on the back as I imagined her face and reaction to this decadent display of my affection. In my imagination, upon seeing all this, her smile would light up the room and her ice queen facade would melt away leaving a soft and grateful woman behind. All these thoughts made that little triangle of nylon seem to shirk and I had to readjust myself so as not to scare my wife into taking one look and run screaming from the room!! With this torture device threatening to cripple me at any moment I slowly made it to the kitchen, where I sent a text warning my oldest that she was to go straight to her bedroom to avoid her being mentally scarred for life.

Putting the now chilled champagne back into its presentation box, I added a cut down red rose and grabbing two flutes I somehow made it to the bottom step of the stairs to await my wife's return.

To pass the time my 'glutton for punishment' mind kept bringing up images of my hands rubbing over my wife's petite frame which in turn had me squeezing shut my eyes and saying aloud "dead kittens, dead kittens, dead kittens" and when that started to fail "Margaret Thatcher, Margaret Thatcher, Margaret Thatcher naked!" and I was truly grateful when I heard the wife's car pull up. My daughter coming thought the door first looked at me standing on the bottom step in my dressing gown shook her head then headed past to the kitchen. My wife had made it into the porch and opening the side cupboard to put away her shoes exclaimed "whose lit bloody candles in my new front room?" Swallowing hard and noticing that her angry tones had worked better than images of dead kittens or a naked Margaret Thatcher had.

As she walked into the hallway she looked me up and down stopping at the champagne, rose and glasses. It was here that I thought her frozen heart would melt but no to my utter dismay she said "MOVE...mind out of my way...I need a pee!" and with that she barged past me and dashed up the stairs. My daughter who had hung around to see this romantic gesture looked at me with pity and I, unable to get my head round it, said "I saw that going differently in my mind". I walked in a daze into the front room wondering where I had gone wrong. Was all my effort for nothing? Was she now immune to my charms? It was at this point the door flew open and my wife now clad in only her underwear leaned back on the door to shut and it said "Well?" Pointing to the blanket I asked her to lie down and as she got herself comfortable I undid the champagne. As the cork shot out we both ducked and I for one was glad it missed us as turning up to A&E in our underwear wasn't something I could have faced.

There she lay on her front eating the strawberries and chocolates, sipping her champagne while looking round the room at the flower and candles. "This is nice", she remarked then spotted the body cream "What's that?"
"That my love is your treat" I said as I stood up and threw off my dressing gown. Thinking back now I have no idea how she didn't choke on her treats or spray champagne everywhere and have put it down to a strong stomach and a bloody good poker face, and my inner insecure man is truly grateful.

Starting at her shoulders I rubbed in the body cream and massaged her body from top to toe, only stopping for a short break, when my hands went into spasm with cramp. Drinking and eating the treats, I carried on. After over two hours I thought I had done enough to earn this ladies favour so to speak and was going to give her the best thirty seconds of her life, only to find her fast asleep. Highly tempted but unwilling to leave her there; I thought it would be a nice gesture to carry her up to the bedroom. However on standing up I found the couple of glasses of fizz had gone straight to my head and as the room started spinning I could barely manage to get myself across the floor. This rusty knight was well oiled! Grasping the settee for support, the best I could manage was to nudge her a few times with my foot until she came round enough for me to beg her to help me up the stairs to bed safely.

And who was it that said romance was dead…?

ABOUT THE AUTHOR

David Glass - usually to be found driving a 7.5 ton truck through towns and villages. Never in a million years did he think that he would be referred to as an 'author'.

This has made this section particularly difficult to write, combined with the fact that many of the details of his life are actually to be found documented in very fine detail in the chapters!

"How did this all start?" I hear you cry. Well we bought a motorhome and shortly after, joined a motorhome group on Facebook. I wrote a little ditty about a great weekend in Nan the van and the rest is history as they say.

My ramblings can often be found on my Facebook group - Brown Trouser Moment Camping with Nan.
I would love to see you there!